Wittgenstein

A graduate of Yale University and holder of a doctorate from Columbia University, **Henry Le Roy Finch** was a professor of philosophy from 1952. His last post was Professor Emeritus of City University, New York. He also authored two companion volumes *Wittgenstein: The Early Philosophy – An Exposition of the "Tracatus"* and *Wittgenstein: The Later Philosophy – An exposition of the "Philosophical Investigations".* He is survived by his daughter, Anne.

The Spirit of Philosophy Series

"This series of books offers the core teaching of the world's greatest philosophers, considered for the light their writings throw on the moral and material crises of our time. Repositioned in this way, philosophy and the great philosophers may once again serve humankind's eternal and ever-new need to understand who we are, why we are, and how we are to live."

Jacob Needleman, Ph.D.
Series Editor

In the same series

THE SPIRIT OF PHILOSOPHY SERIES

Wittgenstein

by Henry Le Roy Finch

vega

A catalogue record for this book is available from the British Library.

ISBN 1-84333-119-5
Printed by CPD Wales, Ebbw Vale
Cover design by Andrew Sutterby

© Vega 2001

Published in 2001 by
Vega
64 Brewery Road
London N7 9NY

Visit our website at
www.chrysalisbooks.co.uk

Acknowledgment is made to the following publishers: Basil Blackwell for permission to quote
from *The Blue and Brown Books; Lectures and Conversations on Aesthetics, Psychology and
Religious Beliefs; notebooks 1914-1916; On Certainty; Philosophical Grammar; Philosophical
Investigations; Philosophical Remarks* all by Wittgenstein; Routhledge & Kegan Paul for
permission to quote from the *Tracitus Logico-Philosophicus*, University of Chicago for
permission to quote form *Culture and Value;* and the University of California for permission to
quote from Zettel.

CONTENTS

Dedicated to all the Wittgenstein students in my classes over the years

What I am writing here may be feeble stuff. . . . But hidden in these feeble remarks are great prospects.

Wittgenstein, *Culture and Value*

Preface

Why didn't Wittgenstein make himself more easily understood? The question itself shows a misunderstanding. It is like asking why one age cannot understand another or one civilization another. Wittgenstein made no bones about the fact that he was out of sympathy with his own age and was writing for a few friends scattered here and there, and for a time that had not yet come.

He expressed himself with the greatest clarity, as students soon find out. Philosophic obscurity was not the problem. And, indeed, the luminous clarity of his writing is one of the main things that convinces students that they have to deal with a great philosopher *even if they do not understand what he is saying*. (Right here we have another myth: that everybody can understand everybody if they try hard enough.)

Wittgenstein knew that it was pointless to try to make himself understood by those who, for whatever reason, could not understand. Not only pointless, but sometimes even damaging, for initial prejudices might even lead to serious misrepresentations. He had twice been the victim of misunderstandings on the part of some of the most intelligent of his contemporaries—once when members of the Vienna Circle of logical positivists, whose position was diametrically opposed to Wittgenstein's (they were exponents of *scientism*, that is, scientific metaphysics replacing religion), claimed Wittgenstein as one of their own, giving rise to an impression of him which could not have been further from the truth. The second time was when, later in life, a writer in *Mind* magazine declared that Wittgenstein's later philosophy was a "linguistic therapy." Wittgenstein knew that he was a "therapist" only in the sense that Socrates was when he spoke to the "sickness" of *his* time. And the sickness of the time Wittgenstein spoke to included overweening faith in psychology and some of its "pseudo-explanations."

The main reason Wittgenstein could not explain himself better was that his philosophy was too innovative to be expressible in the familiar categories his contemporaries insisted upon. In this respect too he resembled Socrates, who was put to death as a Sophist, though Sophism was, in the most critical respect, the exact opposite of what he believed. The few who could understand Socrates had the experience of listening to the stirrings of a whole new age, even the coming age of Christian Europe. He "spoke of the individual soul in a new way."

In this book we attempt to look at what Wittgenstein himself called an *unknown country* with some discussion of how he got there. We do this in two glances—how he came to think about *meaning* (culminating in Chapter 5, "Dimensions of Meaning") and how he thought about *human beings*. The last chapter tries to combine these two into one glance, at a *new way of thinking* in general.

A personal note: When I first began studying and teaching Wittgenstein's philosophy forty-five years ago, I took it as a task to try to make comprehensible to myself and others the main import of his philosophy. I think I have succeeded in making it comprehensible to myself. Whether I have been able to make it comprehensible to others this book will show.

I have to thank my wife and children, who perhaps had more faith in the person than in the task, for putting up with both of us.

PART ONE
What is Meaning?

## CHAPTER 1

Epochal Change

The sickness of a time is cured by an alteration in the mode of life of human beings, and it was possible for sickness of philosophical problems to get cured only through a changed mode of thought, not through a medicine invented by an individual.

Wittgenstein

That some major change in the way we live is beginning to manifest itself is evident from many signs of our times, not the least of which is the exhaustion of the principles by which we have been living. In the midst of continual technological upheaval the sense of emptiness and loss of freedom grows. Unreality and spiritual vacuity spread like a disease. We may recognize in these signs the persistence of certain characteristic problems of the modern age which, if anything, are intensifying: a science which needs neither religion nor morality; a medicine and therapy which cannot deal with the "whole human being" because this conception itself has been lost; a fragmentation of standards and common life; and everywhere the growth of state power, shrinking individuals. These difficulties are reflected in home and street by the spread of violence and drugs and the breakdowns of "twoness relations" on which every culture depends: husband-wife, parent-child, sibling-sibling, doctor-patient, seller-buyer, teacher-student, and, most important, friend-friend. Technology can no longer be controlled or anticipated. The human is overpowered at every level. To say that we have been thinking in a wrong way, a way no longer human, has to be understood not as an empty truism, but as an indication of the change that is in the making.

What kind of change are we sensing or expecting? Nothing, it seems, in the nature of new ideas, new scientific discoveries, or new religions. These could all too easily be absorbed into the existing fragmentation. In a world in which it has become difficult, intellectually and spiritually, as well as even biologically, to breathe, the need is for something quite other than "more of the same." Nor would catastrophes, natural or man-made, necessarily produce the kind of change now beginning.

The change we are speaking about is an *epochal change* that will be at once subtle and all-pervasive. The expressions that come to mind to describe it are *a new way of looking at things, a new way of thinking, a new arrangement of emphases on what is important and not important in human life*. This kind of change has occurred only two or three times in the course of Western civilization—at its beginning in fifth-and fourth-century B.C. Athens, at the beginning of the Christian world in the fourth century of this era, and in the Renaissance of the fifteenth and sixteenth centuries.

Philosophy, even radically changed as we will see it to be, is fundamentally important now, for its task is still to "make sense out of the world" or, as Wittgenstein put it, to help us "find our way about." When, as is happening today, the world in which we find ourselves, and which we ourselves have so largely created, begins to appear unreal, imprisoning the human spirit in arbitrariness, this is the signal that the guiding principles and ideas by which we have been living are no longer adequate and will undergo profound transformation.

We may not expect the change, which seems to be seeping in from many different directions, to be forecast or presaged by any one particular philosopher or prophet. However, the thinker who is attuned to his or her own time as well as to deeper currents may pick up the seismic tremors well before others do and may express some critical formative ideas in advance of the more general historical changes. Such a thinker, in the opinion of many, is Ludwig Wittgenstein (1889–1951), who was born in Vienna, but spent much of his time as an influential teacher of philosophy at Cambridge University, England. Wittgenstein was a thinker of such originality that no one claimed to understand him fully during his lifetime and the attempt to comprehend his "new way of looking at things" and make it available to the mainstream continues. What we do have, and what the present writer shares with a good deal of conviction, is the sense that Wittgenstein's philosophy points the way into the next century and that it is likely to be most influential fifty or seventy years from now.

What can we anticipate in the new epoch if this overall prognosis is correct? The present book will attempt to answer this question, but let me mention here just a few possibilities coming from Wittgenstein's philosophy:

(1) a new conception of the human being in which body and mind and body and soul are more immediately and intimately related than we have realized;

(2) a new immediacy of language and action brought
    about by removing mythical "psychological interme-
    diaries," themselves connected with a wrong con-
    ception of the relation of body and mind;
(3) the recovery of *ritual*, understood as an essential
    part of body-mind connectedness and also as an
    essential element in culture and society;
(4) the gradual disappearance of metaphysics and the
    metaphysical attitude toward science and religion,
    but at the same time a greater awareness of the
    supernatural as directly experienced;
(5) the passing of "psychologism" and "sociologism,"
    through a recognition of their pseudo-scientific
    mythic characters and at the same time their insuffi-
    ciency even as myths.

The End of Metaphysics

What has altered the philosophic landscape in a way
that has not happened since the Renaissance (which
itself saw the beginning of the ascendancy of modern
science as distinct from ancient science) has been the
shifting of the center of philosophic concern from the
question of *knowledge*, or *epistemology*, to the question
of *meaning*. It is a truism that the modern world has
been under the spell of *epistemology*, even as the late
Greek and medieval worlds were under the spell of
Being or *ontology*. That in the twentieth century philosophers of very different schools have turned their attention to the nature of *meaning* as the critical matter, and
what this has done to the rest of philosophy and all our
thinking and understanding, is the first major element in
the epochal change we have been discussing.

While both Plato and Aristotle had characteristic

ideas about the nature of knowledge, the question was given its modern urgency by the development of modern science in the fifteenth and sixteenth centuries. Descartes, in grounding knowledge on the individual thinker and the "clear and distinct ideas" provided by mathematics, framed the rationalist answer, which is at the opposite pole from the empiricist reliance on sense impressions. However, both the rationalist and the empiricist approaches share the characteristic distinction between "subjective" and "objective."

It was the study of *phenomena* (the term *phenomenological* was first used by Kant and Hegel) and of logic and language which led to the central concern with meaning. Edmund Husserl (1859–1938) and Gottlob Frege (1848–1925) did most initially to shift attention from knowledge to meaning—Husserl, as a phenomenologist, concentrating on conscious intentions, and Frege, as a logician, stressing sense and reference in propositional logic. Most important, both Husserl and Frege were enemies of "psychologism," or psychological theories of meaning, which they saw could not satisfy philosophical or logical requirements. (For one thing, the psychologists already have to assume in their own practice what they are attempting to "explain.")

Neither Husserl nor Frege created a philosophy around the concept of meaning. Husserl fell back into Cartesianism, while Frege was never able to integrate his Kantian epistemology with his logical realism. It was left to their followers, Martin Heidegger (1889–1976) and Ludwig Wittgenstein to pick up the essential spirit of Husserl's phenomenology and Frege's logicism and extend them into full-scale systematic philosophies, expressed by Heidegger in *Being and Time* and by Wittgenstein in *Tractatus Logico-Philosophicus.*

It is not surprising that though Heidegger and Wittgenstein were centrally concerned with an entirely new topic, the question of meaning, both at first approached it in terms of the traditional philosophical mode of ontology. Heidegger began his masterpiece *Being and Time* with a question that was completely incomprehensible to Frege and all of those whose primary interest was Logic, namely, *What is the meaning of Being?* Confronted with this question, Frege and Wittgenstein would have said that while it would make sense to ask "What is the meaning of the *word* 'Being'?" it made no sense to ask "What is the meaning of Being?" since nobody seemed to have any idea what the word had to do with it. Heidegger's question would become a little more comprehensible if we translated it as "In what terms can we understand Being as the 'pure transcendence of the world' in its presentness?" The vast range of *Being and Time* deals with the fundamental way of *understanding Being* in this sense. And Heidegger is fully aware that to understand his opening question we have to have what he calls "a vague average understanding of Being" to begin with. This is something like "what surrounds us in the present moment which is not ourselves".

Wittgenstein's *Tractatus*, his initial pronouncement, arrived at its own ontology by asking "What kind of simple essential nature must the world have for a purely logical language (taken to be the essence of all languages) to be able to refer to it and represent it?" The assumption was that this ontology is presupposed by the very fact that language is able to talk about the world (or have meaning) at all.

Heidegger and Wittgenstein were looking for two very different answers to two very different questions, but they were both in search of *absolute grounds*—for understanding and interpretation in the one case, and for reference and sense by structural mirroring in the other. They were assuming, to begin with, the traditional subject-object dichotomy, but in very attenuated ways. For Heidegger, the kind of being human beings have (*Dasein*), and its special relation to time, provide the "opening" that makes Being comprehensible. Wittgenstein's subject attains meaning by "making to itself" *pictures of facts*. That both the *temporality* and the *picturing* have a metaphysical validation shows the extent to which both Heidegger and Wittgenstein were initially within the age-old pattern of metaphysical foundationalism, which posits the human knowing-subject as separate from the world-object.

It is another extraordinary parallel that both of them were unable to carry through their initial philosophies of meaning. Heidegger had to abandon the second part of *Being and Time* when in the 1930s a *turn-about (Kehre)* took place in his thinking, throwing the weight of historical change and initiative on the side of *Being* and not *Dasein*. Wittgenstein announced at the end of the *Tractatus* that anyone who understood him would understand that the framework he had presented made no sense by its own standards and should be discarded (T 6.54). For both men the way was prepared for more radical departures, in which metaphysics would have to be omitted from the start. Would the results still be philosophy?[1]

It is at this point that we begin to look at Wittgenstein as a philosopher of epochal change. And it is important to see that unless traditional philosophy had been summed up and found wanting, this drastic step into a completely unknown realm could not have been taken.

The same thing may be said with reference to Heidegger, who offers an independent and very different alternative to traditional metaphysics (one more closely related to poetry and history) that supplies a supporting counterpoint to what we have to say about Wittgenstein. That the two foremost philosophers of the age should have found their ways independently to *post-metaphysical philosophies of meaning* supports the thesis that this is the direction of philosophy for a coming age.

If, in analogy to the old epistemic question "What takes place in an act of knowing?" we construe a new *question*, "What takes place in an act of meaning?", then the answers first given by Heidegger and Wittgenstein to this second question—namely, the "temporalizing of Being" (i.e., "projects" for the future lived in the present) and the "logical picturing of the world" (i.e., projecting the structure of facts into signs)—both derive their universality and finality from their ontological characters. Epistemology becomes redundant; we don't have to *know* the meaning, we have to *do* the meaning. But it may be also that the two situations are not analogous. Something may be involved in meaning that is not involved in knowing. For Heidegger it will turn out to be *thinking* (what he calls *originary thinking*, which is close to "language-thinking") and for Wittgenstein *ordinary language* (with what he calls its *grammar* or *possibilities of uses*). In the expressions *originary* and *ordinary* we may think we catch an echo of metaphysics or ontology; but Heidegger's *originariness* does not come from the metaphysical stance but from outside it, and Wittgenstein's *possibilities of uses* are regarded by him as just an *aspect* of ordinary language. In other words, the foundational and absolutistic claims of Heidegger's and Wittgenstein's initial philosophies of meaning were abandoned, and this is the decisive step beyond meta-physics into the new philosophical epoch.

What all this means is that before post-metaphysical philosophies could emerge around the concept of meaning, ontologies of meaning had to be tried out, as it were, by both Heidegger and Wittgenstein in their early philosophies. Hence their ontological conceptions of the "meaning of Being" and of "logical pictures" of absolutely simple objects. That both these projects failed, though for very different reasons, is what opened the door to the really new points of view.

Heidegger's much discussed "turning-about" and Wittgenstein's "180 degree turn" both occurred in the middle of their respective lives, and both involved giving up the "metaphysical stance" in which the human knowing subject confronts the world-object. This traditional "humanism," which we attribute to Plato and Aristotle, puts the human being at a confrontational distance from the world, which is seized to be known. As it turned out, this is not the initial stance necessary for either thinking or language. For it may be said, on the one hand, that the world comes to birth in us in thinking, with mutual "presencing," and, on the other, that it is words-act-and-things which are interconnected in occurrences of meaning, though we often also speak of meaning where there are no words and even no acts. What the late Reiner Schürmann said of Heidegger could also be said of Wittgenstein: "To understand Heidegger is to understand that with him philosophy has rid itself of all ultimate *a priori* referents" (*Heidegger On Being and Acting*, p. 123). This may also be described as the "withering away of ultimate representationalism."

The attack on the representational relation to the world (and metaphysics is only the ultimate instance and validation of this) is by no means limited to philosophy. It pervades the arts and sciences. There are many varieties of non-representational art for example, and even what may be called non-perspectival art. In physics the absolute object has disappeared in the quantum theory, and the effects of observation itself have to be factored into what is observed. Both artist and scientist have become, as it were, participants in reality, no longer able to treat the world as autonomously separated. The old absolutely objectified world is no longer a possible starting-point.

Two thousand years of metaphysics, and the absolutistic and exclusivistic "humanism" involved in it, will not disappear easily. The philosopher Nietzsche, writing the last chapter in the history of metaphysics as the *will to will*, prophesied that metaphysics would end in a chaos of nihilism, as all values seemed to give way. This vision itself remained metaphysical, however, since the notion of "relativism" makes sense only in contrast with "absolutism," and if the latter really disappears and does not, as it were, "rule by its absence," the former will disappear too. Yet the transition might involve this absence of an absolute ground as itself the prevailing factor and hence as the "ghost of metaphysics" in somewhat the way that Nietzsche's philosophy itself was. Nietzsche's "eternal return," it seems, was intended as anti-metaphysical, but was not.

The Illusion of Progress

The final heir of the metaphysical tradition, as Heidegger in particular emphasized in his writings on the present condition of technological domination, is what we can call our science, that is, the science which was first developed in the Renaissance as the accepted fundamental understanding of the world (i.e., metaphysical truth) and which has produced in our age electronic communication, atomic bombs, mechanized agriculture, and rocket flight. Conceiving the world in terms of physical forces and rigid mechanical laws has left no room for Plato's Good or anything but mathematical abstractions. The domination of this kind of science, which certainly could be described as "inhuman" or "out of all human sense," is the most characteristic feature of our age.[2]

Wittgenstein pointed this out in a number of incisive remarks, both in the *Tractatus* and in the excerpts from his Notebooks published under the title *Culture and Value*. In the *Tractatus* he tells us that

> The whole modern conception of the world is founded on the illusion that the so-called laws of nature are the explanations of natural phenomena. (T 6.371)

> Thus people today stop at the laws of nature, treating them as something inviolable, just as God and Fate were treated in past ages. (T 6.372)

This superstitious attitude toward the laws of nature (which are in reality only hypothetical descriptions of phenomena) has been accompanied by a belief in the automatic improvement of the human situation by science, or what may be called the dogma of progress. Wittgenstein early on renounced the progressive spirit, which he called the spirit of the modern age, "an age without culture" (CV 8e). The most essential feature of our time was for him an illusion.

> Our civilization is characterized by the word 'progress'. Progress is its form rather than making

progress being one of its features. Typically it con-
structs. It is occupied with building an ever more
complicated structure. And even clarity is sought
only as a means to this end, not as an end in itself.
For me on the contrary clarity, perspicuity, are valuable in themselves.

I am not interested in constructing a building,
so much as in having a perspicuous view of the
foundation of possible buildings.

So I am not aiming at the same target as the scientists and my way of thinking is different from
theirs. (CV 7e)

Apart from the spiritual emptiness of modern science, which takes physical forces in space and time as its
central conception for understanding the universe (and
then wonders why human beings come to be thought of
in the same terms by national leaders), the idea of
progress sacrifices the present to the future by suggesting
that what we cannot realize now may be realized at
some future time when obstacles have been overcome
and problems solved which we are unable to overcome
or solve now. The powerful appeal of such a future-ori-
ented utopianism has been one of the narcotics by which
masses of people have been led to accept miseries and
atrocities now as the price of happiness for future generations. Just as at an earlier time people put a past Golden
Age on a pedestal as a superior time, our age has fallen
into the same illusion, but with regard to the future. It is
perhaps only now after the Communist experience in
Eastern Europe and the increasing savagery of modern
wars that we have begun to understand the way in which
science and technology themselves are postponements of
the critical issues of human life, which always have had

their locus in the present moment. As Wittgenstein succinctly put it:

> The place I really have to get to is a place I must already be at now. (CV 7e)

The notion that the power that has been discovered and released by modern science and technology is *our* power, as if it were at our disposal, is itself an example of philosophical naivete since, socially or "civilizationally" speaking, we have no independent life or identity apart from the whole complex which now contains both the powers and us. We are, as it were, inextricably at one with the scientific and technological powers and do not, as we imagine, merely "make use" of them. Socially speaking, apart from them, we have no reality, and this is why, as individuals, far from being in control of these powers, we feel ourselves to be completely at their mercy. The situation, in other words, moves as a whole, and we have no footing either within it or outside it from which to change it. That the whole moves of itself in a benign direction is the illusion of progress. That we are in control of where it is going is an even more pervasive and deadly illusion.

To speak of an epochal change is to suggest that the whole reality (ourselves and the world in which we live) is undergoing, or beginning to undergo, a transformation similar to what brought it into being in the first place from a previous epoch.

 The Limits of
Logical Language

I have managed . . . to put everything firmly into
place by being silent about it.

Wittgenstein

How Does Language Have Meaning?

There are many remarkable things in Wittgenstein's
Tractatus Logico-Philosophicus, a book that has been
analyzed, debated and examined under the microscope
in scores of articles and books for more than half a century. Although there is much agreement, there is also
uncertainty about even the most central metaphysical
concept in the book, the term *object*.

The book, all will agree, is about "What is the essential nature of the world presupposed by a purely logical
language?" Or "Given the simplest possible language that
could make sense out of the world, what could we tell
from this language about the nature of the world?"
Wittgenstein is engaged in "completing logic" by adding
to it its implied necessary ontological equivalent. In
effect, it is the world reduced to its most abstract minimal

core that is unveiled. It is a world only of facts; all value and ethics lie outside it.

To arrive at this conception of how language has meaning through its most abstract logical essence, Wittgenstein has to deal with a number of subsidiary themes of great importance, which bring him up against the limits of such a logical-factual language and point to what it cannot say. As it turns out, everything that is most important lies outside of it. And this concerns four main subjects.

(1) What language and the world have in common (structure and form or *kinds* of structure) that makes it possible for language to mirror the world cannot itself be said or represented. It can only be *shown* by the identity of the structures (T 4.121). In general what is wholly immanent in language (such as sameness of reference or logical relations between propositions) cannot sensibly be referred to *by* language. There are no metalanguages.

(2) These strictures apply to Wittgenstein's own "metaphysical" language in talking about language (i.e., in describing it as a picture of the logical possibilities of the world). The language that describes facts cannot describe itself. Here Wittgenstein foregoes Russell's hierarchy of metalanguages. *A picture of a picture is still only a picture.* To think otherwise is to indulge in a kind of "false transcendence." A purely immanent logic defeats metaphysics. Russell's approach cannot.

(3) A *genuine transcendence* pertains to ethics and aesthetics and to the "sense of the world," all of which lie outside the world. This is what is truly supernatural or superfactual.

> The sense of the world must lie outside the world. In the world everything is as it is, and every-

thing happens as it does happen: *in* it no value
exists—and if it did exist, it would have no
value. . . . (T 6.41)

And so it is impossible for there to be propositions of ethics.

Propositions can express nothing that is higher.
(T 6.42)

It is clear that ethics cannot be put into words.

Ethics is transcendental.

(Ethics and aesthetics are one and the same.) (T
6.421)

Wittgenstein wrote to his friend Ludwig von Ficker
just after the First World War that the only way to "talk
about" ethics was to delineate clearly the whole area of
facts (what is the case) and then to point to *what is missing* that could *not be talked about*; this would be the
should or the *ethical*. He said that he had done this in his
book.

My book draws limits to the sphere of the ethical
from the inside as it were, and I am convinced that
this is the ONLY rigorous way of drawing these
lines. (Brian McGuinness, *Wittgenstein: A Life*
[Berkeley: 1988], 288)

The key word here is certainly *rigorous*. Wittgenstein's
early philosophy made a god out of rigor or exactitude.
But even when this god was renounced, the ethical still
had a transcendent or supernatural character. Nothing in
Wittgenstein reminds us more of Plato than this 1929
entry in his Notebooks, sentences which, incidentally,
could have been written by Simone Weil, whom he had
not read:

> What is good is also divine. Queer as it sounds, that sums up my ethics. Only something supernatural can express the Supernatural. (CV 3e)

It may sound like Plato, but we should remind ourselves that it also sounds like Tolstoi, whom he had read. Practical obligation, more than prayer and contemplation, has the highest sanction. Religion is directly connected to ethics without, as it were, going through the natural, or the metaphysical. That is the meaning of this from 1929:

> Just let nature speak and acknowledge only *one* thing as higher than nature, but not what others may think. (CV 1e)

What is "higher than nature" is certainly not power or authority, but the source of human obligation or the Good.

(4) The most radical and most difficult themes in the *Tractatus* concern the "truth of solipsism" and the "disappearance of the thinking self." Many a Wittgenstein student must have wished that these topics would go away, but they are indeed an essential part of the Wittgenstein teaching and have a direct bearing on what, as later transformed, relates him most to the future.

Before we can even begin to fathom these ideas we must first of all back up to the strictly structural and formalist view of language (ordinary language only "dresses this up"). Where then lies the direct and immediate experience in the present moment of the content of the world? Wittgenstein's very starting point is that *this cannot get into language.* There is no way of speaking about it; it cannot be referred to; it is truly unspeakable. Think of the color *red* for example. Even if we make the word *red* itself red this will not help, since holding up the color red does not say what I would like to say when, for example, I say: *I mean what I see at this moment when I am looking at that.* "At what?" the other person may say. "At that," comes the reply, pointing at the red patch. "What are you pointing at—a shape, a locality, a surface?" "No, I am pointing at redness." "Once again you give me a word, which, of course, I know how to use. But I want something more."

These are the introductory moves in a philosophical quest where every turn runs into what looks like a blank wall in a labyrinth. There is something we are trying to say that cannot be altogether wrong and yet cannot be altogether right. It is the position of solipsism, summed up in such curious statements as "I am the only one who experiences red (and *all* immediate experience) since I never experience yours and the only thing I know about the world firsthand is what lies in my own field of consciousness at each present moment. When I am experiencing the world this way, it looks as though only I exist or my consciousness. Of course I know this is preposterous since to whom am I talking and what am I trying to tell them?"

Many other questions arise. When the painter Barnett Newman painted a surface as big as a gallery wall bright red and nothing else on it, what was he trying to say? Was it like a shout, "Look! This is what you cannot say or refer to, but also cannot deny or ignore or translate"? It is a strange paradox that what would appear to be the most common, public and accessible world— the world of immediate experience—should be the most private, isolated and inaccessible. The painter Newman's red *means* this.[1] Wittgenstein's philosophy tried to *clarify* the paradox.

The Fly in the Fly-Bottle

The "truth of solipsism" if it could be stated (and it cannot be) would have to be stated "from the outside of one's own consciousness," but nobody can get outside his or her immediate experience (i.e., his or her consciousness); it *has* no outside. So we are unable to say what we try to say with expressions such as "My world is all the world there is," or "I never have anybody else's experience but my own." (The fact that we speak of "losing" and "regaining" consciousness and of states of "half" consciousness and "heightened" consciousness, quite unconcerned about whether it is our own or someone else's, does not bear on these questions of perception or consciousness-of.)

What is, however, inextricably tied up with first-person experience is the present moment. In a sense all experience is experience within the present moment (even if it involves memory or imagination or future anticipations). As Wittgenstein pointed out, however, language takes place in time, and before the end of the sentence is reached, immediacy is gone or replaced by a new immediacy. All the difficulties that attach to the solipsistic situation of the first person (that is, *I*) appear again in connection with the unique status of the present moment. The present appears to be incommensurably real, while no such claim can be made for the past and the future. It is even confusing to say that the present is fleeting, for there is a sense in which it doesn't seem to belong to time at all, the sense in which it is, by contrast with past and future, *real*, however short-lasting that reality.[2]

(It should be noted that this is another place where the orbits of Heidegger and Wittgenstein approach each other, for Heidegger also was centrally concerned with the "mystery of presencing" and finally seemed to identify *Being* with *presencing*.

The topic of solipsism is discussed at great length in the *Blue Book* (1933–34), pp. 44–74 and the topic of the present in *Philosophical Remarks* (1929–30), pp. 80–88. Perhaps the most illuminating discussion of all is in "Notes for Lectures on 'Private Experience' and 'Sense Data'", reprinted in *Philosophical Occasions 1912–1951* (1934–36).

The importance of this topic cannot be exaggerated because it has a close connection to Wittgenstein's thinking about the subject and the self, and later on what he has to say about mental processes and the impossibility of a metaphysically private language. All of this comes under the heading of one of the most far-reaching changes carried out by Wittgenstein's philosophy: the emptying-out of the "inner world" as the main locus of the most valuable kind of experience, not in the interests of a reductionist behaviorism (though Wittgenstein is often at first misunderstood in this way), but of a much more integrated soul-and-body and body-and-world.

The initial step in this direction was his attempt to "show the fly the way out of the fly-bottle," as he put it, which meant to release the solipsistic subject (the totally private subject of modern Cartesianism and Calvinist capitalism) from the trap in the human being. This lonely, isolated, fearful subject has been at the center of Western philosophy since the time of Descartes as, in a sense, the balance to the objectified mathematical universe. Wittgenstein's work was to carry this conception to its logical extreme and *then* to rearrange the entire geography. When we grasp the point that

> what the solipsist *means* is quite correct, only it cannot be *said*, but makes itself manifest.

The world is *my* world. . . . (T 5.62)
I am my world. (The microcosm.) (T 5.63)

Then we see that the subject, any subject, can be *identified* by its world and does not need any special "content" of its own, *qua* subject, which is not and cannot be "world." At this point Wittgenstein can say, in flat rejection of Descartes (and the whole ego basis of modern philosophy),

> There is no such thing as the subject that thinks or entertains ideas. (T 5.631)
>
> Here it can be seen that solipsism, when its implications are followed out strictly, coincides with pure realism. The self of solipsism shrinks to a point without extension, and there remains the reality coordinated with it. (T 5.64)
>
> The philosophical self is not the human being, not the human body, or the human soul, with which psychology deals, but rather the metaphysical subject, the limit of the world—not a part of it. (T 5.641)

Here, in Zen Buddhist parlance, the *goose is out of the bottle*, but not totally because the metaphysical point remains, though this can have no personal identity and therefore no attachments, desires, or anguishes. Otherwise the self is gone!

Here too the subjective source or base of thinking disappears. Thinking takes place, but it is not "done" by an agent, or a private locked-away metaphysical self. It is part of the factual world, as are the soul and body, *or* it is an illusion. Wittgenstein's no-agent conception of thinking leaves us not with Descartes's *Cogito ergo sum, I think therefore I am*, but with *Thinking takes place, therefore I am not.*

Wittgenstein makes a sharp distinction b\
thinking, which he says does not need a subj\
agent, and *willing*, for example, moving one's own l\
which *does* involve agency. If the essential meanin\
thinking is picturing, we can begin to see what he has\
mind. On the other hand, this doctrine leaves us uneasy\
And the uneasiness perhaps turns around Wittgenstein's\
own example of thinking.

Wittgenstein's own philosophical method always
seems to have involved an inner questioning and
answering (though this was hidden by the *ex cathedra*
pronunciamento style of the *Tractatus*), and it is difficult
to understand why he did not see at least the inner questioning as an act of will, though his reply might have
been that the questions "came to him" too, as much as
the answers, and therefore were not, strictly speaking,
his doing. But even if this be admitted, it would seem
that "directing one's attention" is, at least to some extent,
within one's own control, and this is part of thinking. We
will return to this subject when we look at what he later
on had to say about the grammar of the word *thinking*
(which is the correct way to approach this problem).

What is clear enough is that Wittgenstein's discussion of solipsism (paralleled in sheer unrelenting tenacity
only by Samuel Beckett's discussion of the related topic
of personal identity in *The Unnamable*) is one of the
most profound approaches to the problem of the self to
be found in philosophical literature, East or West. We can
compare it to the thought of the Buddhist-oriented
philosopher, more readable, but also far less profound
and far-reaching, Arthur Schopenhauer. As it happens,
Schopenhauer was Wittgenstein's first philosophical reading and may well have been his introduction to the subject of solipsism.

Schopenhauer's main work, *Die Welt as Wille und Vostellung* (*The World as Will and Idea*, 1819), begins with the notorious sentence "The world is my idea." We all know what he meant, but his philosophical naivete in leaving it at that and in a way building his whole system of thought on that must have left Wittgenstein somewhat aghast. Should not the next sentence have been "Whom are you telling this to then, and how could they (not being you) possibly understand it"? And with these additions the fat is in the fry.

Wittgenstein suggests, perhaps half-humourously and without applying his words to Schopenhauer, that we might be willing to "accept this notation" (i.e., let the philosopher talk that way) and agree that the world is Schopenhauer's world without being so rude as for each of us to make the same claim for him or herself (which would be to be as absurd as Schopenhauer was). But what would be accomplished by this, except to humor the philosopher? Philosophy is full of such insults to common sense; this is only one of the most outrageous of them.

What makes Wittgenstein a great philosopher is that he really does try to seize the nettle, sting and all, and hang on to it for years, in this case trying to find out what made Schopenhauer say such a thing and how it could be reconciled with common sense. That the problem is ultimately that of the "fly in the fly-bottle," or releasing the human self from its self-imposed prison, makes it not just a philosophical problem, but also a religious and civilizational one. That Wittgenstein was ultimately successful in solving this we will see in Part II of this book.

## CHAPTER 3

Breaking the Spell of the Ideal

> I think now that the right thing would be to begin my book with remarks about metaphysics as a kind of magic.
>
> Wittgenstein

The most severe criticism of the *Tractatus*, and therefore the greatest help in understanding it, came from Wittgenstein himself in the first part of his second major work, *Philosophical Investigations*. He lived to free himself from the rigid system of his first book and in doing this to deliver the most penetrating criticism of the logical ideal it enshrined. It was only because of the intensity with which he had embraced the cause of logical exactitude that, in renouncing it, he was able to bring the metaphysical commitment which sustained it down with it.[1]

The core of the scientism that Wittgenstein had always rejected (that is, the "metaphysicalizing" and "religionizing" of science) lay in the absolutizing of mathematical logic, which he accepted, and the former could not be really undone without undoing the latter. The logical absolutism of the *Tractatus* was not the answer to the idolatry of science, but, as he came to realize, something more like its last, purest expression. When he reduced the intelligibility of the world to pure logical objects (rather like generalized geometric coordinates in different kinds of "property spaces"), he was carrying to extremes the scientific project to mirror the world in the most abstract, value-free terms possible. If that failed, then "our science" failed too. In other words, as long as the logical ideal of total rigor and total exactitude (so beautifully expressed by Wittgenstein's mentor Gottlob Frege) held sway, and with it the idea of a universe that could be "grasped" in that way (a universe real just in that "graspability," despite its entirely accidental factual character as to just which of its logical possibilities existed or did not), then just so long would our civilization persist without "true culture."

This is why we have to look closely at just *what* Wittgenstein rejected when he rejected his own early philosophy and *why* he rejected it.[2]

The Prison of Logic

Wittgenstein had argued, with an intellectual force that "nearly knocked people down," for a gospel of icy-cold logical purity, purity of absolutely simple names and absolutely simple objects, of isomorphisms between corresponding structures of these objects and names, and finally for the generation of *all possible complex propositions* by a single operation of *General Negation* (T 6.01) (a conception which he later described as *making a god out of Negation*). Simplification by abstraction could not have gone further. There was something awe-inspiring in the sheer perfection of it. What could possibly have persuaded Wittgenstein to give it up? After this *how could he* and *why would he* settle for a pluralistic and "ordinary" and non-systematic conception of the world and language? If we did not have a full account by Wittgenstein himself of the change, it seems to me that we would not have been able to imagine it. And perhaps if the beginnings of the change had not been made in the *Tractatus* itself, the change would not have been possible.

Wittgenstein came to believe in time that in his *Tractatus* years his mind had been held in one rigid position, looking fixedly in one direction and unable to look around. He had been mesmerized by an ideal conception of logic, by a dream of perfection, or what seemed like perfection, of a singularly monostatic sort. The mind frozen in the metaphysical stance, never before so clearly seen.

Suppose that the absolute determinateness that it seemed must lie at the heart of the world was instead a requirement imposed by the logician, perhaps not even a requirement that made any sense, like "All roads must go somewhere," or "There must be a smallest of all objects." We might instead imagine a different standard like *sufficient unto the context is the exactness thereof*, the exactness of a railroad time-table not requiring the use of seconds, as is needed in athletic running events, or the millionths of a second of the physics laboratory.

Wittgenstein described what he had been doing in the *Tractatus* as "subliming the logic of our language," "subliming" here meaning "absolutizing," by creating *super-objects* and a *super-subject* to match *super-names* and *super-concepts*. (The analogy to the larger-sized gods shown in the Egyptian tombs, carrying on the same activities the humans do down below, but bigger up above, can hardly fail to strike us.) The metaphysical notion of a geometrical point having no parts and hence being completely simple here exercises an irresistible appeal if we want *ultimate* reference. The fixed ideal seems to have the greatest reality, and to be the most indispensable.

> The ideal, as we think of it, is unshakable. You can never get outside it; you must always turn back. There is no outside; outside you cannot breathe.— Where does this idea come from? It is like a pair of glasses on our nose through which we see whatever we look at. It never occurs to us to take them off. (PI 103)

The *a priori* order of the world, the order of possibilities, *must* be there—this is a feeling which testifies to the hardness of the logical necessity. What seems inconceivable is that the world itself should not contain at bottom this perfect order.

> Thought is surrounded by a halo—Its essence, logic, presents an order, in fact the a priori order of the world: that is, the order of *possibilities*, which must be common to both world and thought. But this order, it seems, must be *utterly simple*. It is *prior* to all experience, must run through all experience; no empirical cloudiness or uncertainty can be allowed to affect it—It must rather be of the purest crystal. But this crystal does not appear as an abstraction; but as something concrete, indeed, as the most concrete, as it were the *hardest* thing there is. (PI 97)

Wittgenstein at one point told a friend that to get out of philosophical tangles it is necessary first to have been immersed in them or to immerse oneself in them. This was his own experience in relation to the entirely gripping mind-set of the *logical must* and its supposed ontological equivalent. He had been in that prison and knew first hand how escape-proof it was.

This *Tractatus* rigidity imposed by the "picture of the picture" was actually portrayed on canvas by the French surrealist painter René Magritte. One of his paintings shows a canvas on an easel, and on this canvas is a painting of a landscape, the very landscape that it stands beside, which is visible through the window next to the easel. Here is depicted the reflecting nature of pictures (reminiscent of the famous "hall of mirrors" in fun fairs), which, if we give it a "logical" character, or add to it the logical "must," is exactly the way Wittgenstein imagined the *world, thought* and *language* to line up in reference to each other. The pictures were structural, made up of points in different kinds of property spaces, rather than of paint on canvas. Otherwise Magritte has portrayed the Wittgenstein conception of "pictures mirroring pictures."

When he had escaped from this conception, Wittgenstein himself gave a striking metaphor to illustrate the way the *Tractatus* had looked at the world. He said the writer of the *Tractatus* was like a man imprisoned in a room, sitting on a chair facing a blank wall on which he imagined doors and windows through which he vainly tried to get out. Repeatedly he tried these doors and windows unsuccessfully, but then suddenly realized that *all the time a door behind him had been open.* This discovery, we may say, corresponded to the realization of the *manifestational, expressive*, and *performative* character of language, which was just as important as its "picturing" character and could also be "described," once we broadened the meaning of the word "description." We cannot escape through metaphysical doors and windows (rigidly supposed to be only in front of us), but there is no more prison after we find the door *behind* us.

Wittgenstein had been in the grip of the "metaphysical stance," which, he saw now, requires getting "in front of" everything, that is into the position of "looking at"— *even our own subjective experiences*, for example, as Wittgenstein discovered, even our own *pain*. If we would "look in the opposite direction," we would discover these happenings to be clearly *manifestational*, which means something we *cannot* "get in front of" or "see in the mind's eye." As we will see when we talk about Wittgenstein's "abolition of the inner facade," when we attempt to "objectify" in these cases, the result is only illusion and metaphysical frustration.

A further important aspect of the *Tractatus* was its completeness and finality. It was a definitive formulation that claimed to be the *only possible* setting forth of the *a priori* nature of logic and its implications. Wittgenstein believed that he had settled these questions once and for all. That there could be some other possible way of understanding logic and its relation to the world was not conceivable. Or at least it was not conceivable until in 1928 he heard three lectures by the distinguished Dutch mathematician L. E. J. Brouwer, who held to a very different philosophy of mathematics along the lines of a Kantian "intuitionism" where the sequence of numbers in arithmetic was taken as more fundamental than geometrical structures. This gave rise to a whole different basis for both mathematics and logic, which put the emphasis on finite constructions rather than infinite logical space. Wittgenstein was suddenly confronted by an alternative: that his own previous way of looking at logic and mathematics was *not* the only possible one.

Family Resemblance:
Naming and Meaning

Wittgenstein's later philosophy of logic and mathematics was based neither on Frege's and Russell's *calculus of logical relations,* nor on Brouwer's *successiveness of human consciousness,* but rather on the kinds of *common agreements that make cultural life possible.* When he said that a "six-year-old child knows as much about the foundations of mathematics as Bertrand Russell does," he meant that learning that "two plus two equals four" is learning an application that has the widest ramifications in human life, the denial of which in practice might well qualify one for a mental hospital. We do not need any stronger "necessity" than that, but it will help us if we realize that in learning such a simple arithmetical truth, we are not learning some "truth" about the world or some metaphysical order underneath the world, but are learning an agreed-upon "measuring stick" like "twelve inches in a foot." "Convention" does not mean "arbitrarily subject to anybody's will"; it means "as deeply woven into the structure of human life as anything could be." In giving up what he came to see as the "logical mania" of the *Tractatus,* Wittgenstein was renouncing a certain kind of necessity, but what replaced it was a no less strong necessity and one which had its applicability built into it. A very different world would doubtless have found a very different arithmetic expedient, but still no "truth" would have been involved.

The change of thinking, having many aspects, freed Wittgenstein from the logical fixation of the *Tractatus,* and carried with it a rethinking of many smaller fixations. These included "normalizing" or bringing back to ordinary usage such words as *names, concepts,* and *sentences,* all of which he said are "sublimed" by logicism.

The idealized logical conception of *naming,* or how a name is set up and functions, imagines an inner psychological act of naming *per se* in which the human mind performs a kind of occult operation of attaching a word to a mental object (as it were "baptizing" the object), this act being the means by which *this* word now gets *that* meaning. Wittgenstein points out the emptiness of this supposed performance, which by itself accomplishes nothing.

> We may say: only someone who already knows how to do something with it can significantly ask a name. (PI 31)

Names have many uses, such as calling things to mind or identifying them or pronouncing a word when something is pointed at (PI 31). The supposed *psychic act* accomplishes nothing without these uses.

Wittgenstein now faces a more general problem, another requirement which seems to have given way— that concepts should have definite and clearly bounded meanings, each concept only applying to all the things that have a particular definite feature in common. For example, the concept *name,* as a concept, might be thought to get its meaning from being properly applied only to all those words which stand in the exact naming relation to objects. Or we might take the word *picture* as this is used in common speech, or the word *game* (which is Wittgenstein's new preferred metaphor for language activities). In ordinary language is there any one thing that all pictures must have in common to justify that concept being applied to them? For example, if

a photograph is too fuzzy to make out what it is supposed to be a photograph of, do we call it a *picture?* Or
a caricature of someone we do not know or recognize?
Or a Christmas design? It will be hard to find any common denominator for all the things called *pictures*. The
boundaries of the concept will appear arbitrary or
blurred. And so too with another example, the concept
game. When we see the actual range of what are called
games, we will give up imagining that they all have *anything* in common (PI 68, 70).

> "But if the concept 'game' is uncircumscribed
> like that, you don't really know what you mean by a
> 'game'."—When I give the description: "The ground
> was quite covered with plants"—do you want to say
> I don't know what I am talking about until I can
> give a definition of a plant? . . . "But is a blurred
> concept a concept at all?"—Is an indistinct photo-
> graph a picture of a person at all? Is it even always
> an advantage to replace an indistinct picture by a
> sharp one? Isn't the indistinct one often exactly what
> we need? (PI 70–71)

The acceptance of blurred concepts as being wholly
workable in ordinary life without needing the underpinning of total exactness (unless this has to be *constructed*
for some specific purpose) leads Wittgenstein to a new
way of thinking about conceptual similarities or how
concepts function in general. This is the idea of "family
resemblances." Speaking of what justifies the use of the
word *game* for all the phenomena we call "games," even
if there is no single feature in common, he says:

> I can think of no better expression to character-
> ize these similarities than "family resemblances"; for

the various resemblances between members of a
family: build, features, colour of eyes, gait, temperament, etc., etc., overlap and criss-cross in the same
way.—And I shall say: "games" form a family. (PI 67)

The "common features" conception of essence, and
of what therefore concepts must correctly apply to when
we use the same word to speak of any member of a
group of objects, goes back to Plato's Socratic dialogues,
where a correct definition is sought, usually for ethical
concepts, and Socrates takes for granted that there is one
and only one "defining essence"; since this can be found
for everyday occupations we have a right to expect that it
can be found for abstract ethical terms, like *justice, love,*
and *piety,* too. If the search for the "common feature"
turns up anomalous features, the assumption is that the
word in question is incorrectly applied in these cases. On
the other hand, Wittgenstein compares *family resemblances* to thread which is made by twisting fiber on fiber,

And the strength of the thread does not reside in the
fact that some one fibre runs through its whole
length, but in the overlapping of many fibres. (PI 67)

This is the way it is, for example, with the concept
of *number* or the concept of *language* or the concept of
meaning (as we shall see). (Different kinds of "numbers"
in mathematics have nothing in common!)

In the Fitzwilliam Museum in Cambridge, which
Wittgenstein must have visited many times, there is a
well-known painting by one of his favorite painters,
William Hogarth. It shows simply the faces of about six
or seven members of the same family. Looking closely at
this painting, we can easily see what Wittgenstein meant
by "family resemblance," for indeed we do not see a

single common feature in the faces, but there is nevertheless a marked (and I would say *haunting*) similarity
between them all. We would say, "Yes, they are all members of the same family," even if we had not been told
that they were. When we look closely however, we are
not able to pin down any single feature common to all.

Can the word *essence* be retained when its age-old
meaning of "class nature" or what is named by a "class
name," a meaning subsisting through the Middle Ages
and down into modern times, has been abandoned? Is
there any similarity between the old meaning of *essence*
and the new one that would justify continuing to use the
same word? (The question is rather like the one whether
Wittgenstein's later philosophy should still be called "philosophy." Here the usage of philosophers seems to have
settled the matter. The question has been raised, in an
even more pointed way, with respect to Heidegger's later
philosophy.)

What is the common usage of the word *essential?* It
is certainly fuzzy enough. One can pick up a book on
education, for example, or cooking or crime and come
across a sentence like this: "The essential elements are
so-and-so." The meaning seems to be "most important"
or 'indispensable" but without implying anything "defini-
tional." It is a form of emphasis. In books where classifi-
cation is more important we might expect groupings to
be introduced according to a family resemblance principle, and the degree of exactness of definition would
vary, as Wittgenstein says it does, depending on the subject matter and the speaker's or writer's intentions.

Philosophy, however, as we shall see in the next
chapter, has a special interest that makes the words
essence and *essential* particularly important for it. In trying to get a clear view of the world and of language it

especially concerns itself with the *possibilities* of both. This was the central concern in the *Tractatus* where the *a priori* order of the world was an *a priori* order of *possibilities.* When these were no longer seen as logical possibilities but as grammatical ones, they nevertheless remained possibilities, and this concern continued to separate the philosopher's interest in language from the scientist's (i.e., the linguist's), *even after the possibilities no longer had a metaphysical or ontological status.* The linguist studies language as fact, the philosopher as possibilities. The linguist wants to develop hypotheses and theories (more or less accepted hypotheses); the philosopher wants to arrange (or rearrange) the possibilities of meaning in order to get an overall sense of the "lay of the land." Wittgenstein said that for him clarity was an end in itself, not aimed at some further result (CV 7e). This is a statement that has enormous cultural and religious implications.

People who share the point of view of the *Tractatus* when they search for the *essence* of language are looking for "a final analysis of our forms of language, and so a *single* completely resolved form of every expression" (PI 91). Wittgenstein says that he too is "trying to understand the essence of language," but for him this is "something that already lies open to view and that becomes surveyable by a rearrangement" (PI 92). In the one case the essence is hidden from us and has to be, as it were, dug out by an abstracting reductive process. In the other the uses of words are accessible on the surface, but we have been misled into confusing different types of uses; therefore we must clear up the confusions (the philosophical problems) by seeing which expressions and forms of language properly go with which others in the ordinary usages that are the home of all these meanings.

## CHAPTER 4

Grammar as
Deep Culture

We must plough over the whole of language.

Wittgenstein

The chief terms in which Wittgenstein's new way of
thinking is expressed are *grammar, language-games,
forms of life,* and *natural history.* To acquaint ourselves
with his most important later ideas we have to familiarize
ourselves with these terms.

The first thing to notice is that they are not metaphysical (hard as it may be for some philosophers to
accept that central terms in a philosophy need not be
metaphysical). Wittgenstein makes it clear that these are
not to be understood as super-concepts, that he is not
departing from the ordinary meanings of *grammar* and
natural history, and that *language-games* is a metaphori-
cal expression, set up to "serve as a measure" or to provide "*objects of comparison*" (PI 130). (All ideals, he says,
should function thus, but language-games are not ideals.)
The most cryptic expression, *forms of life,* which he
never fully discussed, has given rise to considerable con-
troversy, which we will examine.

A second point to notice is that these terms, in a distant way, parallel the key terms of the *Tractatus*, as if they were something like transformations into a totally different key. Thus *grammar* replaces *logic, language-games* replace *logical pictures, forms of life* replace *logical structures* and *forms*, and *natural history* replaces the *world of facts* as seen by *natural science*. If we imagine these terms arranged in two parallel columns, the one might be called the column of *abstract reduction* and the other the column of *descriptive rearrangement*. Both aim at universality, the one by way of abstract generality, the other by bringing into view what users of language already know in their own use.

Grammar: Description of Essence

We might say that between the two stages of Wittgenstein's philosophy *essence* and *description* change places. Whereas in the *Tractatus* he is after the *essence of description* (which is also the essence of language and the world), in the *Philosophical Investigations* he is after the *description of essence*, where essence is the phenomenon of language seen in the *aspect* of possibilities for meaning and sense. And whereas the *essence of description* is logic with its ontology, the *description of essence* is the description of ordinary grammar.[1]

When G. E. Moore objected that Wittgenstein was using the word *grammar* in a special way, Wittgenstein replied emphatically that this was not so and that when he spoke of "philosophical grammar," he meant by "grammar" the same thing as when the word was used in *Grammar* School (that name and that kind of instruction).

Grammar may be called the "essence of the world" in the new sense of "essence," and philosophy is the "custodian of grammar" (PR 85). This means that "grammar is the shadow of possibility cast by language on phenomena" (PG 329). It tells us what kinds of things things are (PR 74) and gives language the "necessary degrees of freedom." Instead of being the abstract heart of language, grammar is an aspect of language, the aspect that concerns the philosopher because it deals with the *possibilities* of language.

Most important are two points: that grammar consists of *conventions* (PG 138) and thus has a cultural context, and that grammar is *autonomous* and not beholden to any other reality.

> Grammar is not accountable to any reality. It is grammatical rules that determine meaning (constitute it) and so they themselves are not answerable to any meaning and to that extent are arbitrary. (PG 184)

Because grammar is autonomous, like arithmetic, which is the "grammar of numbers" (PR 23), it *guarantees its own applicability.*

These are, in a way, the deep features of grammar, or the particular aspects of language that concern philosophers. But language also plays a vast variety of tricks on us, which generate our philosophical problems and which can be cleared up only by getting a clear view of the uses of our words (i.e., of the grammar). At every turn we encounter tricks, difficulties, and confusions from misunderstanding this deeper grammar.

How does language work its power over us to mislead us? There is a long list of ways in which it tempts us to misunderstand it. Wittgenstein mentions, for example, these:

—suggesting misleading pictures (PI 140, 305, 397; BB 43, 115)

—surface similarities concealing deeper differences (PI 109, 132, 187)
—suggested analogies that can't be carried out (BB 28, 49)
—leading us to try to say what cannot be said (PI 119)
—entangling us in our own rules (PI 125)
—conflicts between different uses of words (PI 26)
—creating out-and-out illusions (PI 100–10)
—giving incorrect accounts of uses of words (PI 345)
—inventing a myth of meaning (PI 374)
—counting some useless thing as a proposition (PI 520)

These kinds of mistakes that we are "tempted" to make are the "raw material of philosophy" (PI 254), what philosophy attempts to clear up by gaining a clear view of what goes wrong.

Sometimes we have to do with more than temptations. Pictures, words and grammar "force themselves on us" (PI 397, 178, 304); pictures "hold us captive" (PI 115), or we are "unable to turn our eyes away from them" (PI 352) or we "have an urge to misunderstand" (PI 109). There is a "fascination" in misleading analogies (BB 26–7) and a "bewitchment" we have to resist (PI 109).

The paradox of language is that, on the one hand, grammar represents the normal, average intelligence of human beings as this has been culturally funded in the *a priori* patterns of usage of language, but, on the other hand, we are constantly being misled, deceived and confused by misunderstanding these normal workings. Language cannot be "explained" or "justified." It doesn't need to be "grounded." It doesn't even need to be "applied"; it is applicable by its very nature. In its possibilities it is *a priori*, but not unchangeable and not beyond all happenings, nor independent of human history and doings.

Grammatical remarks, as the philosopher advances them, we should understand clearly, do not report facts of usage (this belongs to anthropology or linguistics), but *possibilities* of usage, which are the *binding norms* of a language, conventional, historical and changing, but nevertheless necessary and presupposed. In them, as it were in a common currency, we see the meanings of a culture. But never all at once, for they come to our attention only when normal functionings go askew. Then we find ourselves in the grip of pathologies of language, which lay hold on us as powerfully as any mental or physical disorder.

Language-Games

This general way of looking at depth grammar may itself mislead us into thinking that grammar by itself will tell us about meaning. But the matter is more complicated. Wittgenstein asks:

> Is the meaning only the use of words? Is it not the way this use interlocks with life? (PG 65)

And the *Philosophical Investigations* does not begin by talking about grammar, but by talking about *language-games*.

Before we look into the question of what a language-game is, we should notice one fact of central importance, that the *unit of meaning* here already involves in one complex the three factors of *human beings*, a *world-setting* and *language*. So far as I know, this is the first time in Western thought when the starting point for thought was not, in however disguised a way, a subject and object, which a philosopher then attempted to relate to each other. We have taken *that* as the root human situation, as indeed, for example, the *Tractatus* did, laying down the simple objects, the metaphysical subject and the epistemic relation of logical picturing. This is the epistemological (knowing starting point), which we have been also calling the "metaphysical stance."

In understanding the *Philosophical Investigations*, nothing is more important than recognizing as a *beginning* what would never before have seemed to be even a conceivable beginning. Wittgenstein students who keep trying to push Wittgenstein's later philosophy back into the old mould fail at this point: they cannot conceive that anything as apparently complex as what Wittgenstein called a language-game *could be a starting point!* But it is precisely Wittgenstein's genius to have seen that the *initial unit of meaning* has to be an interrelation of this kind of a triplicity, and that nothing less than this will do. (It has long been a dream of philosophers to get out of the subject-object starting point, but the possibility of this was understood only "mystically.") That we could simply see meaning itself as already in its simplest form "before" this dichotomy had not occurred to anyone. Charles Peirce perhaps came the closest, but his "threeness" was put forward as on a par with "firstness" and "secondness."

Wittgenstein's famous initial example of a language-game is one which has come to be called *The Builders* (PI 2ff). After an opening paragraph quoting St. Augustine about how he learned language, Wittgenstein begins his book with this:

> Let us imagine a language for which the description given by Augustine is right. The language is meant to serve for communication between a builder A and an assistant B. A is building with building-stones: there are blocks, pillars, slabs and

beams. B has to pass the stones, and that in the
order in which A needs them. For this purpose they
use a language consisting of the words "block", "pil-
lar", "slab", "beam." A calls them out;—B brings the
stone which he has learned to bring at such-and-
such a call.——Conceive this as a complete primitive language. (PI 2)

Most important here is the "completeness" that we
are asked to "conceive." Wittgenstein deliberately chooses a "command" situation (which is not the *Tractatus*'s
picturing) and something that looks like "naming" (but is
not the kind of "naming" we had in the *Tractatus*), and
also "sentences" (which are not like the *Tractatus* sentences). Here is a "primitive language" whose simplicity
defies the *Tractatus* kind of simplicity. It is "primitive"
(not "logically simple"), in the sense that it might,
Wittgenstein says, be the "whole language of a tribe" (a
point that has been disputed), but also "primitive" as
being like "one of those games by means of which children learn their native language" (PI 5, 7). Wittgenstein
then also introduces a critically important ambiguity: the
expression "language-game" is to refer to the language
itself but

I shall also call the whole, consisting of language
and the actions into which it is woven, the "language-game". (PI 7)

Many critics have questioned the possibility of
"imagining" any such language as "the whole language of
a tribe." Surely if these people had a language this complicated, they would make provisions for mistakes or the
assistant not hearing, etc., and furthermore if they had
such *buildings* to begin with, would they not "know"

more about building itself than their four command words allow?

It is hard to see just how serious these objections are. He does seem to discount them when a little later he says that the "language-games" he is talking about are not intended to be real but are only set up as "objects of comparison." The point is to call attention to certain salient features rather than reproduce a natural situation.

> The term "language-*game*" is meant to bring into prominence the fact that the *speaking* of language is part of an activity, or of a form of life. (PI 23)

(Here appears the very important expression *form of life*, which we will be discussing in a moment.) Then follow the fifteen examples of what Wittgenstein means by a "language-game." Our first real understanding may come from this list.

> Giving orders and obeying them—
> Describing the appearance of an object, or giving its measurements—
> Constructing an object from a description (a drawing)—
> Reporting an event—
> Speculating about an event—
> Forming and testing a hypothesis—
> Presenting the results of an experiment in tables and diagrams—
> Making up a story, and reading it—
> Play-acting—
> Singing catches—
> Guessing riddles—
> Making a joke; telling it—
> Solving a problem in practical arithmetic—

Translating from one language into another—
Asking, thanking, cursing, greeting, praying. (PI 23)

How many such language-games are there? An indefinite number. And new ones are constantly coming into being and others disappearing. As we proceed and give other examples, these "simple" meaning-units will become more comprehensible.

The Natural History of Human Beings

Before we look at this list to see what we can learn from it we should note that Wittgenstein draws a line under it and tells us that these language-games arise out of even more primitive natural behavior, which he describes as the *natural history of human beings.* This includes:

> commanding, questioning, recounting, chatting, are as much a part of our natural history as walking, eating, drinking, playing. (PI 25)

It is Wittgenstein's view, hinted at here, but expressed more directly elsewhere, that human culture including language arises out of natural history. (He is cautious about formulating this because he does not want to open the door to theories, e.g. Darwin, as to how this might have happened since such theories are not the concern of philosophy and, in addition, quickly become fodder for myths and ideologies.)

Not all languages make use of words, not even all human languages. Some use numbers (arithmetic) or gestures (rituals) or sounds (if we think of music as a language), etc. And when we think of animal languages, the list is much longer. (Bees, ants, birds, and chimps have all been studied in detail.) Wittgenstein regards human spoken language as being part of human natural history, not to be *explained*, as natural science mistakenly attempts to do, giving rise to the plethora of "explanations which do not explain" so familiar to us.

To return to the much discussed list in PI 23, we can see how the examples he has chosen might be thought of as the germs of law, physics, architecture, history, causality, scientific theories, literature, pretending, words set to music, humor, mathematics—to mention only some obvious connections.

It seems clear by now that the last example, bringing together "asking, thanking, cursing, greeting, praying," refers to what Wittgenstein would describe as the ritual (or ceremonial) use of language. And it is perhaps significant that all five of these activities (with the possible exception of the last one) occur in both secular and religious contexts. And this helps us to answer such questions as, "Is 'religion' one language-game or many?" for it seems clear that every religion embodies many different language-games, for example, praying, confessing, reciting, responding, chanting, sermonizing, memorializing, prophesying, sacrificing, divinizing, baptizing, confirming, marrying, consecrating, anointing, blessing, sanctifying, venerating, etc.

This helps us to see that the examples given in Wittgenstein's list are intended only as samples, and no doubt each item could be expanded into a larger cluster of related language activities. Under the heading of *giving orders*, for example, might be put such things as instructing, demanding, contracting, protesting, licensing, permitting, scolding, examining, exhorting, codifying, swearing-in, testifying, witnessing, etc., etc. Here are many activities connected with the law, authority and rules, and with military, educational, and political life.

In the next chapter we will see, however, that the situation is by no means as chaotic as this may make it appear. Although all these language activities qualify as language-games, they can be classified into four main directions or dimensions without resorting to abstraction or reductionism.

Forms of Life

What must concern us first, however, is the relation between *language-games* and *forms of life*. In all of Wittgenstein's writings (now running to fifteen volumes in the projected edition covering writings from 1929–1933 only, and easily twice that if covering all the rest), there are only nine occurrences of the expression *form of life*, five of them in PI. All of these passages have been most illuminatingly discussed by Newton Garver in a recent book *This Complicated Form of Life* (Chicago, 1994), and we will return to one of his main points in a moment. The most important of the nine texts, I think, is this one:

> It is easy to imagine a language consisting only of orders and reports in battle.—Or a language consisting only of questions and expressions for answering yes and no. And innumerable others.——And to imagine a language means to imagine a form of life. (PI 19)

The form of life he is talking about in the first case is war, for that kind of exclusive language activity is indeed what happens on the battlefield, and in the second a legal trial and what happens on the witness stand. It will be helpful if we think of a form of life as a certain kind of activity, more or less regularized in human life (or animal life), leaving aside such questions as whether it is cultural or biological or both and how limited or universal it is.

To imagine a language (here Wittgenstein does not use the expression *language-game*) *means to imagine a form of life.* But to this is added a page or so later:

> Here the term language-*game* is meant to bring into prominence the fact that the *speaking* of language is part of an activity or of a form of life. (PI 23)

We may expect from this we could list side-by-side language-games and forms of life and in this way come to see what Wittgenstein means by both these terms. I choose some modern as well as ancient examples.

language-games	*forms of life*
advertising	buying and selling (commerce)
psychoanalysis	therapy
	(dream interpretation)
haruspicating	divination
betting on lotteries	gambling
exorcism	magic ritual

We gather from these examples that a form of life is necessary to give full sense to a language activity. Suppose, for example, that an anthropologist sees a group of women down by the water in the morning arranging themselves in a particular order while carrying what appear to be clothes. Is this laundry or a religious purification or both or neither? We need to know not only what they are doing but also a wider context of how it fits into other activities in their lives if we are to understand the language that accompanies their activities. The form of life does not *explain* the language-game, but it does make it comprehensible. It distinguishes, for example, a ceremony from a daily chore, even though the two may at times overlap.

There appear to be certain words and certain phenomena and activities connected with them that are of
such a character that we could not limit their use to any
particular form of life, but might have to describe their
form of life as the whole of human life. And this, I take
it, is what Newton Garver is dealing with in his book
already referred to, particularly in his chapter "Form of
Life" and the section entitled ". . . this complicated form
of life" (252–4). Here he is discussing the most puzzling
of the Wittgenstein references to *form of life*, which reads
like this:

> Can only those hope who can talk? Only those
> who have mastered the use of a language. That is to
> say, the phenomena of hope are modes of this com-
> plicated form of life. (If a concept refers to a charac-
> ter of human handwriting, it has no application to
> beings that do not write.) (PI p. 174)

Garver feels that the "complicated form of life" referred
to by Wittgenstein in this passage must be the complete
human being and cannot be (as I had suggested in an
earlier book) the "activity of hoping" or "phenomena of
hoping." While I now think that he is right, the matter is
greatly clarified if we see that the language-game with
the word *hope* (no doubt as with other words not given)
is part of a form of life that is of the whole human being,
while various other language-games such as the ones discussed above are connected with limited human activities. In other words, as Wittgenstein uses the term,
human life as a whole may, in connection with certain
words, be a form of life, while in connection with other
words more limited activities constitute the necessary
meaning-context.

This suggests that, unlike *language-games, forms of*

life may include each other, in the sense that, as a "complicated form of life," the human form of life includes other forms of life such as war, business, education, religion, etc. The one mistake we must not make is to try to squeeze the form of life concept into such terms as *culture, biology,* or *history.* It is obvious that Wittgenstein wants this phrase to be as flexible and wide-ranging as possible, certainly to the point of its *being usable at different levels of generality.*

Something of the same thing applies to the other key term *natural history,* a phrase that enjoyed greater prestige in the eighteenth century, brought back into prominence in this philosophy. We have to see this against the background of Wittgenstein's repudiation of modern natural science, not only for its usurping of the place of religion, but for its pretentiousness and self-inflating, or allowing itself to be inflated into myth-making and ideology. Wittgenstein's reaction to the atomic bomb in 1946 expresses this succinctly.

> . . . the bomb offers a prospect of the end, the destruction, of a dreadful evil, our disgusting soapy water science. (. . . die Bombe das Ende, die Zerstörung, eines grässlichen Übels, der ekelhaften, seifenwässrigen Wissenschaft, in Aussicht stellt.) (CV 49e, 49)

The cutting off of science from the Good, which occurred in the Renaissance, paved the way for a science that reduced everything to mechanical forces to be exploited by human beings. Wittgenstein saw the true "dreadful evil" not as being the Bomb, but the science that produced the Bomb, which is very much still with us.

What are the advantages of *natural history* over *natural science,* as Wittgenstein sees them? They come down to one central teaching: what Wittgenstein regards as the superiority of *description* to *explanation*. Like many others, he was sick with the surfeit of *explanations* in the modern world.[2] Theories, systems, ideologies, alleged causes, points of view, beliefs—they multiply like rabbits. And the proposed solutions to our problems make the problems worse. As Thomas Szasz said of psychoanalysis: "It is itself the disease which it sets out to cure." This could be said of many proposed "solutions," which are on the same level as what they purport to have the answer to.

We remember the *Tractatus* conception of "pure description" as isomorphic structural mapping. Even after dropping this he still held to the idea of philosophy as "purely descriptive" and containing "nothing hypothetical." But now the word "description" was broadened to its everyday usage while being "focused" on the description of grammar, a word that was said to "guarantee its own applicability." Wittgenstein gave three examples of such words that "guarantee their own application": *geometry, arithmetic,* and *grammar.*

With such words we do not need to worry about their applicability; we do not have to take it into account. The applicability of grammar is not something additional to grammar. Consider a child learning "two plus two equals four"; the very learning shows what to do with the expression. (In a colloquy with G. E. Moore, Wittgenstein imagined a situation in which the formula would *not* apply: if every time we tried to join two objects with two objects one of them, as we would now say, unaccountably disappeared, we might prefer an arithmetic in which "two plus two equals three.")

Like arithmetic, grammar is autonomous, cannot be "explained" and does not itself "explain." But it can be described by the philosopher, and these descriptions, which are of normative everyday meanings or uses, will straighten out philosophical dilemmas brought about by misunderstanding these everyday usages. We will see in the next chapter that Wittgenstein has to "demythologize" or straighten out the concept of *following a rule* and *meaning* as involving *following rules*, while, on the other hand, no such difficulties surround the word *use* since this does not so easily give rise to false pictures making the grammar of the word *use* a nightmare of "false turnings." *Use*, of course, is not to be understood teleologically or pragmatically (much less psychologically or culturally); everything we need to know about it we will learn from examining the role it plays in our everyday speech. In this matter, as in geometry and arithmetic as well as in art and aesthetics, "Since everything lies open to view, there is nothing to explain" (OC 182).

CHAPTER 5

Dimensions
of Meaning

Language can be observed from various points of view. And they are reflected in various concepts of "meaning".

Wittgenstein

It is misleading to call Wittgenstein's later philosophy a "system" since he thought his *Investigations* "only an album" of "sketches" put together after sixteen years of "criss-crossing" an unknown terrain. When the highly systematized *Tractatus*, with its algebraic abstraction of modern logic, mathematics and sciences broke down, a modest piecemeal campaign of forays took its place.

For the moment it looked as if Wittgenstein's effort to understand meaning in one comprehensive look had been abandoned. If there would be no more attempts at *exact* definition, would there be any kind of definition at all? All we could grasp was that he was talking about ordinary usages of language, in a way having started all over. The meaning was in the use, but this was not the whole story, for he said:

> For a *large* class of cases—though not for all—
> in which we employ the word "meaning" it can be
> defined thus: the meaning of a word is its use in the
> language. (PI 43)

What about the other cases? Can we get a glimpse of the
full range of meaning of the word *meaning* here? This is
what we undertake in this chapter, taking a step beyond
where Wittgenstein left us.

We begin by looking at four main conceptions of
meaning, or aspects of meaning, which Wittgenstein
emphasizes and discusses in various places:

(1) *Meaning as Rule-Following* (PI 54, 84, 130)
(2) *Meaning as Use* (PI 43, 132; PG 60)
(3) *Meaning as Custom* (PI 19, 23, 90–1, 241)
(4) *Meaning as Physiognomy* (PI 536, p. 218)

These four main emphases jump out at us from the pages
of Wittgenstein, but just how they are to be related to
each other he does not say. In trying to keep them all in
mind at once (essential to Wittgenstein's kind of understanding) I have found it indispensable to put them in
the following arrangement, in a diagram related to both
the human body (top and bottom, right and left sides)
and to the four points of the Compass.[1]

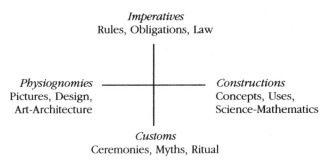

To complete the diagram we follow Aristotle in suggesting that the vertical line be labelled *Doings* and the horizontal line *Makings*. The horizontal line requires a balance (perhaps of left and right brains?), but so also, I want to suggest, does the vertical line if we are not to fall into some kind of dominational reading. In our time all the weight has been thrown on the upper right-hand quadrant, the right-hand "constructional" point of the Compass, at the expense of the other three "dimensions," and this imbalance goes a long way toward defining the "sickness of our time." We cannot speak of the whole human being except in the sense of giving *equal weight to all four points of the Human Compass.*

Looking at the diagram and imagining "language possibilities" at the center, we might visualize it this way:

To make this more concrete, imagine a town in which there has been a bad school-bus accident. A sign appears on the City Hall, *Day of Mourning,* for this is the *custom,* and it will involve certain *rituals.* Signs that are understood as *Commands* also appear, saying *No Parking.* And there are pictures of both the Mayor and the Governor, normally happy looking, but now everyone can read their faces as having very sad expressions. Finally there is a proposal to build a Bus Safety Memorial at the scene of the accident. Nothing is particularly unusual here, given what happened, but the story brings out the four different kinds of meaning—the custom (form of life?) of community mourning, the commands or rules reaching down to automobiles, the expressions on the faces of the people, and a "constructional" response. Since all of these meanings intersect and overlap and there are a good many complications and details which we have ignored, the diagram gets its strength more from our sense of its being anchored in the concrete individual human being than from its being derived from cultural or social situations.

Even though Wittgenstein discussed the use (concept-forming, mathematics and science) "point on the Compass" more than any other (it being the dominant point in *our* lives), he also devoted considerable space to "Meaning is a physiognomy" (PI 568), to *seeing* and *seeing as* (PI Pt. ii), to "following rules" (not only in PI but in the writings on mathematics) and to the subject of ritual (in the *Remarks on Frazer's "Golden Bough"*). In Chapter 10 of this book, contrasting the philosophic methods of the *Tractatus* and the *Philosophical Investigations*, we look into the question of the deeper implications of the mistake of putting the right-hand point of the Compass at the center of the whole.

When we examine in more detail each of the four points or dimensions of meaning, we can begin to see how they complement each other. When we do this, we will see how and why each of the Four Points on the Human Compass (the phrase is mine, not Wittgenstein's) has to be "restored" by being understood fully and brought back into balance with all the others before we can speak of the "wholeness" (or even the full sanity) of the human being again. And we will also see why *language* has to be placed at the center as the fulcrum for the proper "balancing" of each of the two human axes. (It is also important to avoid the "psychologism" of putting one of the traditional "subjective" factors at the center, which is certain to be misunderstood.)

What is wrong with the world, in the Wittgenstein point of view, can easily be seen if we try putting the Right or West point at the Center. This would be an apt illustration of what we call "scientism" (and incidentally can only be done by continuing to "metaphysicalize" science). The Soviet Communist alternative comes into view when we try putting the North or Command point in the Center and keeping it there by force. The symmetrical alternative to this is putting the Custom point at the Center and, in turn, maintaining it there by force.

All four of the Human Compass Points have to be "recovered" together to permit the equal "balancing" of Left and Right, East and West, Art and Science, and also of Head and Body, North and South, Law and Custom, Doings and Makings. Two "axes of balance" are involved. Wittgenstein's philosophy shows this can only be done in terms of the centrality of Language, the only alternative to some form or other of "psychologism," "sociologism," or "historicism."

There is a proper way of thinking about each point on the Human Compass that gives it its "normal" place and weight in the whole configuration. But until we have seen and used this "normal" place in relation to the rest (and not to the exclusion or "inferiorizing" of the rest) we do not have the whole picture. It is everyday language with its philosophical grammar that permits us to do this, for this is indeed the "Archimedean point," empirically transcendent without being metaphysical, from which the whole can be seen.

We start with the Left or East side of the Compass, the Seeing or Picture Side. From his earliest writings in the *Notebooks 1914–16* to his last work on *Philosophical Investigations Part II*, Wittgenstein never stopped being concerned with the "meaningfulness of seeing." His friend and executor Elizabeth Anscombe in her early (1959) book *An Introduction to Wittgenstein's "Tractatus"* said that it sometimes seemed as if the whole world was a Face which Wittgenstein looked at. In other words things had meaningful "expressions," which could be read off directly from the appearances without the intervention of "psychological" (or better, "psychologistic") interpretations or explanations. The human face, with its absolutely crucial importance to us, was the paradigm for all such physiognomic *meaning-seeing*. (See the chapter on "Physiognomic Phenomenalism" in my book *Wittgenstein's Later Philosophy*.)

This conception that the face of the world, the appearances of the world, are self-revelatory (i.e., deliver their meanings directly to the right kind of looking) was something Wittgenstein shared with Goethe, who saw nature this way, as "expressive phenomena".[2] It is also what distinguished Wittgenstein from the Gestalt psychologist Wolfgang Köhler, whom he read. Wittgenstein, unlike Köhler, believed that we *see meanings* and not merely "*organizations*" to which we then *add* meanings. It is axiomatic with Wittgenstein that meanings cannot be "explained"; they have to be *read off* from phenomena or brought into clarity by conceptual "rearrangement" of grammar, by cultural empathy (in the case of strange rituals) or by reminding us of what we normally do or say.

In his very important sections on "aspect-seeing" in Part II of PI where the notorious duck-rabbit picture served as a model, Wittgenstein separated himself from art perception theorists such as Erwin Panofsky and quantum physicist theorists such as Norwood Hanson, both of whom, in completely different contexts, defended the position that "all seeing is *seeing as*." Wittgenstein was able to avoid falling into this trap through his conception of Grammar, for Grammar told him that there is a useful (and "plenty good enough") distinction between *seeing* and *seeing as*. We do not, for example, say, "We see those table utensils over there *as* a fork and spoon" (unless there is some special reason to talk that way). We say, "The fork and spoon are already on the table; I see them there." This is a good example of Grammar that has to be straightened out, the difference in usage between *seeing* and *seeing as*, in order to avoid the kind of pitfall that two such learned men as Panofsky and Hanson landed in. A "metaphysical picture" misled them, and only the normal intelligence of ordinary language could help us set the matter aright.

In many ordinary situations of life we see things as directly meaningful and do not have to go through some psychological operation to put *meanings* into them. An unnecessary psychological dogma is getting in the way. The "starting point," which we should not try to reduce or put in some other terms, is meaningful perception. No abstract theory or myth can, by metaphysical *lèse-majesté*, improve on this. (In a more current mythic mode we have only another example of "left brain domination" over "right brain," reversing the "handedness" that rules in the body.)

We move now to the second point of the Compass—the North or Imperative, Head-Rule-Law point, which brings us to what Wittgenstein had to say about "demetaphysicalizing" (or demystifying) rules and rule-following. Since Grammar concerns itself with getting clear about grammatical rules, we have to begin by trying to get clear about rules themselves, and about rule-following (the paradigmatic kind of action at this point on the Human Compass). What is involved here will also affect rule-following in mathematics. We must not accept the picture that makes it seem that all the steps prescribed by the rule are somehow already present, as if magically foreshadowed, in a super-necessity reflected in or embodied in the rule itself.

Suppose to generate the number series we have an operation *Add one*. It is sufficient that by habit and practice we do what we usually do. In order to break the hold of the idea of some further super-necessity involved here, Wittgenstein points out that we *could* if we wished do it differently (and, as it were, get away with it, and even justify it), calling what we do *Adding one*. A learner doing "adding one" might proceed thus: 1, 2, 3, 4, 5, 6, 7, 8, 9, 10, 12, 14, 16, 18 etc., and when told that he had not done it right because he had switched to " 'adding' *two* after reaching the number 10," might reply, "I thought that what I did was what you meant, that when there are two digits, 'adding one' *means that*. What I did was not wrong; it was just another permissible interpretation of what it is to 'Add one'." If this person stuck to his guns, Wittgenstein's point is that there is nothing, in heaven or earth, that could "rationally" override him, except arguments about convention and convenience. There is no "metaphysical content" to a mathematical or grammatical or any other rule.

Many people have argued against this, including the American philosopher Saul Kripke.[3] Can Aristotle's Laws of Thought, which generations of philosophers have told students have a metaphysical status—for example, "Something cannot both be and not be the case in the same sense at the same time"—be given a Wittgensteinian deep conventional interpretation? Suppose somebody says (the example is Wittgenstein's) "You cannot both sit down and stand up at the same time," and I maintain that I am doing it when I sit on the very edge of my chair with half my weight on my feet and the other half on my rump. The rest of the conversation can be imagined: "But that's not what I meant!" "But that's what the sentence you uttered means," etc. To which the reply will remain, "That's what *I call* 'sitting down and standing up at the same time'."

From this we can conclude that no rule or operation or command could be formulated with such unequivocality that someone (a madman, a drug addict, or just a stubborn philosopher) could not defeat it by just hanging on "past the point of all reason," though he will surely also argue that what he is doing is what *he* calls "reasonable."

Are we simply surrendering to an unheard-of relativism, breaking down all decent limits of civilized discourse? Not at all! We are refusing to be bound by a particularly narrow conception of reason. Wittgenstein once formulated his position this way: Intellectual necessity is something that we always have the option of not going along with. Even Euclid: "If A is larger than B and B is larger than C, then A is larger than C." But if a noncommutative algebra, in which "2 times 3 need not equal 3 times 2" is possible, so too is a non-transitive geometry. (The fact that neither of these has any daily use points to just where the necessity of mathematics really lies. The normal human intelligence embodied in normal grammar is also to be found in normal arithmetic and in preferring what is self-applicable in ordinary life.)

In our rapid trip around the Human Compass we

move on to the Right Side, the Western Side, now the dominant point of the Compass in our present world civilization. Wittgenstein was right to single out *construction* as the key word, meaning not only the construction of concepts, which is what mathematics and science do (consider the creation of different kinds of numbers and number systems in the history of mathematics), but also the use of these concepts in technological building. (It is no accident, too, that one of the supreme artists of the twentieth century, Marcel Duchamp, should have thought of himself as a *conceptual artist*, while some forty or fifty years later *conceptual* became a key word in international politics because of its employment by people like Henry Kissinger.) Wittgenstein distinguished himself from the spirit of his age in the following quotation in his Notebooks:

> Our civilization is characterized by the word "progress". Progress is its form [i.e., what is taken for granted—ed.] rather than making progress being one of its features. Typically it constructs. It is occupied with building an ever more complicated structure. . . .
>
> I am not interested in constructing a building, so much as in having a perspicuous view of the foundations of possible buildings. (CV 7e)

Construction is a good word for our technological civilization, dangerously unbalanced to the top right-hand quadrant of the Human Compass, unable to find the right balance, politically, genderly, culturally, or geographically, and as a result torn by internal conflicts. Its "building" gets bigger and bigger and more and more out-of-control because the rest of the "human image" is missing. Left and Right tearing each other apart and no one able to find a Center is a fair enough political version. And our chart shows these two to be essentially interchangeable like the two sides of a seesaw, defined only in their supposed difference by the myth of progress.

Wittgenstein describes concepts as *tools* and *instruments*, which have definite uses and applications and which can be employed for building intellectual (e.g., financial, corporate, ideological) structures, as well as the technological physical equivalents in vast cities, highways, dams, etc.

At the bottom of the Compass, backward and seemingly unimportant, is the repository of tradition, custom, cultural roots and, centrally it seems, what is most impossible for us today (though it surrounds us in unseen forms on all sides), ritual. Wittgenstein was very much aware of the importance of ritual, abhorred it when it was dead, but put nothing above it when it was spontaneous and alive. (The present writer experienced such a living ritual when a young child: having been told of the glory of a great tree in New England, on seeing it he rushed forward and kissed it.) Dead, empty and mechanical repetitions (which is the way many people think of religious rituals) should be contrasted with very much alive, but intrinsically far less important national and patriotic rituals. It is worth observing also that the two most ritualized forms of human life have been two of the longest lasting: the religious and the military. This makes us all the more concerned to understand the nature of ritual.

What needs to be said first is that ritual is body-language. Wittgenstein was, as usual, entirely on target when he said that he could easily imagine a religion without word-language. If we think of the Hopi Snake Dance (so brilliantly described by D. H. Lawrence in

Mornings in Mexico), or the initiation "sightings" at Eleusis in Greece, or the Roman Catholic Mass, or the religious processions in Italy, or the Mayan human sacrifices at Chichén Itzá, or the Celtic May Day Beltane Festival discussed by Sir James Frazer in *The Golden Bough* (and by Wittgenstein in his thoughts on this)—if we think of all of these, we will get an idea of the universality of ritual and the way it is linked to the human body. We are not surprised to find out how important are *gestures* (saluting, waving, crossing, genuflecting, bowing, etc.) and *body positions* (kneeling, lotus position, prostration, blessing, etc.) Spoken words, singing, chanting, howling, shouting, and readings are also often integrated into ritual, so that even word-language appears in ritual aspect.

Rituals of everyday life (blending into customs and conventions) which are so pervasive that we don't even notice them are often thought of simply as "good or bad manners." From the way people stand in conversations, social distances, tilts of the head and directions of gaze, a great deal can be learned, not to mention different ways of sitting, walking, and turning the body and head. Books discuss the "Language of the Fan" in eighteenth-century Europe as well as in ancient China and Japan, and every period has its language of fashion and body decoration. It seems to come naturally for people to describe these activities and manifestations as "languages," perhaps because of the similarities with spoken language. The concept *language*, of course, has "broad edges." Everyday spoken language is the "common currency."

Having boxed the Compass to examine the four main aspects of language as Wittgenstein saw them, we turn to one more overall look at it, this time in terms of the four aspects of Logic, followed by a diagram of the Reflexivity of Language.

The Logical Compass

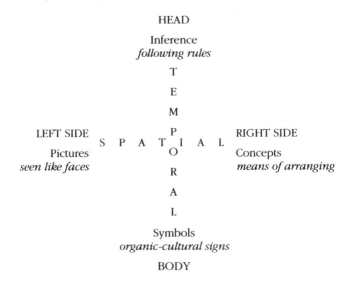

The difference between *concepts* and *pictures*, in a kind of horizontal balancing, and *rules* and *customs*, in a vertical one, seems to justify this diagram, if we are to take in these four very different concerns, all of which interested Wittgenstein, altogether as it were in a single glance. The perspicuous view of logic, once we no longer see it confined to the upper right-hand quadrant, would seem to dictate this grouping, which may then have both a pictorial and symbolic significance.

The final *map* concerns the reflexivity of language itself, or the way in which language works on itself in accordance with the four points:

The Reflexive Language Compass

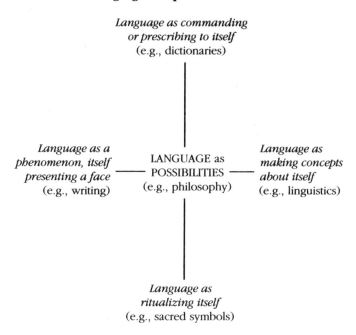

Language as commanding
or prescribing to itself
(e.g., dictionaries)

Language as a
phenomenon, itself
presenting a face
(e.g., writing)

LANGUAGE as
POSSIBILITIES
(e.g., philosophy)

Language as
making concepts
about itself
(e.g., linguistics)

Language as
ritualizing itself
(e.g., sacred symbols)

This chart shows the "layering of determinations" by which language itself illustrates its own four main aspects (beginning at the top and proceeding clockwise):

(1) in dictionaries—it defines itself;
(2) in linguistics—it creates concepts to theorize about itself;
(3) in religions—it sacralizes itself;
(4) in writing—it gives itself a face.

The extent to which this reflexivity almost threatens to overwhelm us (each one of the four points being applicable to the other three if we simply widen it slightly)

shows the importance of having a strong central symbol
(like the Compass and the Human Body). But we can see
how fragile, nevertheless, even this symbol is if we consider that each of the four corners can be applied to the
whole chart as it sits on the page above. Thus, the entire
chart is made up of *concepts*, while altogether they are
put in the form of a *picture* or *diagram*, which *instructs*
us how to take it on the basis of a *customary* understanding of compasses and the human body.

These reflections should serve also another purpose,
which is to show how impossible it would be for anyone
to understand this chart, by approaching it in the
abstract-precision way of thinking of the *Tractatus*.
Unfortunately some of Wittgenstein's most articulate
commentators fall into this category of trying to understand the later Wittgenstein philosophy in the same way
that we try to understand the earlier. (The opposite mistake occurs also: that people familiar only with the
Philosophical Investigations are unable to make head or
tail out of the *Tractatus*. And there is a striking parallel
for the partisans of the two different phases of
Heidegger's philosophy.) The difference in method
between the two phases of Wittgenstein's philosophy is
the subject of the last chapter of this book.

PART TWO
New Image of the Human Being

 Relocating the Self

> A whole mythology is deposited in our language.
>
> Wittgenstein

There is an uncanniness about Wittgenstein's philosophy, with which teachers and students (and there have been, and are, many hundreds of courses, especially in English-speaking countries over the last fifty years) are very familiar. Generations of philosophy students have become familiar with his work and have experienced the same curious sense of studying something that they know neither they nor their teachers fully understand; yet they know, with the same kind of certainty, that it represents something of enormous importance, just slightly beyond their grasp. They leave college, in many cases, with a lifelong devotion to something that is more than a mystique or a cult, something, it seems, just over the horizon, whose beautiful glow has just begun to reach us.

This feeling has nothing at all in common with what young people may feel about "cyberspace" or coming wonders of technology. It is much more than a hope, and certainly has nothing special to do with religion or the occult. It is something powerfully immanent, worth a lifetime of study to try to understand, though few will go that far, something that belongs to the future, even if we are not able to say yet just how or in what way. This sense of futurity connected with Wittgenstein's philosophy cannot be gainsaid. One purpose of this book is to coax this Wittgenstein future out into the open, where it will be eventually. (If this "making Wittgenstein available" is not successfully done here, it will be elsewhere.)

It has become more and more clear that the "uncanniness" and the "irresistible movement" are most connected with one particular aspect of Wittgenstein's philosophy, one to which he devoted by far the most attention. And it is precisely with regard to this area that the future is so strongly on Wittgenstein's side.

Abolishing the Inner World

What has to be done, and what Wittgenstein knew has to be done is to make the same turn-around with regard to the so-called "inner world" (i.e., the situation of the human subject in its relation to its own "mental contents") as he had made with regard to outer objects when he abandoned the rigid "frontal" metaphysical stance, although here the problem would be even more difficult since there was no "one answer for all." It would be necessary to go through the major "psychological-philosophical" concepts one by one and by scrupulous examination of the language-games involved show that none of them function "psychologically," but only "grammatically." The target is to get rid of what I have called in an earlier book on Wittgenstein the "inner facade" of

Western thought. And this work is what we find in two-thirds of the *Philosophical Investigations*: a careful examination of what have been regarded as "mental" phenomena and concepts (PI 134–427): *"fitting," understanding, reading, knowing how to go on, rules, private sensations, thinking, images* and *imagining, I-consciousness-soul.* This is followed by an equal space (PI 428–693) devoted to the "intentional" aspects of mental phenomena and concepts.

To go to the heart of the matter, we may say that Wittgenstein worked to abolish the *inner world, but by no means the inner life.* For him, getting rid of the former begins *to make real the latter.* Wittgenstein's greatest achievement was that he overturned the assumption of two millenia of Western thought that an "inner world" of the subject has to be constructed on (and can be justified by) the model of the metaphysicalized objective world. An objectified "internality" has been taken for granted, particularly since the time of Saint Augustine; we have the same thing, merely secularized, in Descartes and, in another greatly changed form in the presuppositional "transcendental psychology" of Kant. There is no way of coming to grips with the "psychological taint" in philosophy without coming to grips with the erstwhile "inner world." The "inner world," however, has had great prestige. By being connected with "spirituality," it has had both a philosophic and religious significance. The spirit (which can never be objectified) gained a certain weight and prestige by being connected with the metaphysical through this "inner world." But at the same time it lost what is infinitely more important, its ever-renewed *inner aliveness.*[1] The importance of this distinction between the "inner world" and the "inner life," which we have never, before Wittgenstein, been able to separate in mainstream philosophy, will become more apparent as we proceed.

The usual procedure in dealing with Wittgenstein's hundreds of pages of "philosophical psychology" in which grammar dissolves, concept by concept, the "inner world", is to discuss this "destructive" aspect first and then to add, almost as an afterthought, the role of the inward spirit in Wittgenstein's own philosophic method and practice.

In order to see that there *are* two sides to what Wittgenstein is doing (what he writes about and what he demonstrates) I propose to reverse the usual procedure and speak first about what, strictly speaking, cannot be spoken about—because of the danger of once more "objectifying." It is demonstrated on almost every page that Wittgenstein's philosophical method was an inner dialogue with himself, consisting of posing questions and inwardly "listening" to answers. But this had a peculiar character because, as he says in his Notebooks, these questions had to be asked in a state of complete inner detachment, probably not too far from the "released" (*Gelassenheit*) state described by Meister Eckhart and made pivotal in the later philosophy of Martin Heidegger. Wittgenstein described it as each morning "going down into chaos" to find again the living germ.

> Each morning you have to break through the dead rubble afresh so as to reach the living warm seed. (CV 2e, 1929)

> When you are philosophizing you have to descend into primeval chaos and feel at home there. (CV 65e, 1948)

In light of this (and indeed this is just what is demonstrated in every line of Wittgenstein's philosophy in its originality and newness) we can see how absurd it is to describe Wittgenstein as a behaviorist. It further goes without saying that Wittgenstein knew very well what he was doing, and how he was doing it.

Wittgenstein was indeed engaged in a destructive task, but what he was tearing down was the 2,000-year-old "inner facade," metaphysically produced assumptions about the subject's relation to itself, some of which, we discover, have become so taken for granted that they pass for common sense.

The sweep and scope of Wittgenstein's innovation in destroying what he called the "house of cards" of the "inner world" becomes evident when we realize that every single Western philosopher since Plato has accepted in some form or another the conception of *mental contents of the mind or consciousness* (as has every modern psychologist). All have assumed the *existence of* images, ideas, thoughts, impressions, notions, concepts or the like. (The only exceptions, of course, are modern behaviorists, who have never been taken seriously by philosophers and are not by Wittgenstein.) As one contemporary historian of philosophy has written:

> Certainly the most influential doctrine in Western philosophy which professed to explain the relation between language and thought is the doctrine that there are concepts or ideas which constitute a medium between the cognizing agent and the things which are known.[2]

Plato, Aristotle, Anselm, Aquinas, Occam, and since the Renaissance both rationalists like Descartes, Spinoza and Leibniz and empiricists like Locke, Berkeley, and Hume have all accepted the assumption of mental contents to serve as "objects" of such supposed mental activities as *knowing, perceiving, imagining, believing, thinking,* and *intending.* It never occurred to anyone that it just might be that there are no such "mental objects." This seemed unthinkable, if only perhaps because the "inner objects" seemed necessary to supplement and back up the outer objects if we were to begin with that kind of a separation. In a very attenuated form Wittgenstein himself had subscribed to the very same idea of thoughts being some unknown somethings in the mind. At this point he did not doubt that there were images existing in the mind though of what nature they were he could not say (T 2.13).

It is this entire doctrine of mental contents that Wittgenstein, on the basis of grammatical analysis of the ordinary so-called "mental" words involved, came to see as an unnecessary duplication, a kind of mythical intermediary between subject and object, separated almost as if to give rise to just this mythical connection between them. In the first instance he was out to destroy the Augustinian-Cartesian "inner object of knowledge," the strange "duplication" by which we not only experience, feel, and think but also *seem to know what* we experience, feel, and think, as well as the very processes which *seem* to be involved in all of this. The "duplication" in Wittgenstein's view is the result of multiple misunderstandings of language which give rise to this odd picture.

From this Wittgenstein goes on to question and disperse such "transcendental *schein*" or "transcendental mirages" as the inner mental contents. He shows what many of us have long suspected, that *thinking, understanding, reading, meaning, intending, believing* are not mental processes at all. (The way these words function shows this, and the student can look into any one of them he or she chooses in PI through its Index). He also shows what we have *not* suspected: that none of these are "mental activities" or "mental happenings" of any kind at all. And, as we will see, even such image-laden activities as *memory, perception,* and *imagination* are part of the same mirage of the inner facade.

The Myth of Mental Process

The most obvious, and in some ways most practically harmful, expressions of the "inner facade" are notions like these: that if we are to speak sensibly, some mental process, voluntary or involuntary, must take place first, for we feel that speaking doesn't just happen by itself, though Wittgenstein's point is that *it indeed just does*; that when we "obey an instruction" or "follow a rule" the mind has to go through some process of "understanding" first, again our feeling being that it couldn't just occur, though Wittgenstein's point is that *it indeed does just occur*; that recognitions or identifications are either themselves mental happenings or require mental happenings to be able to take place, but Wittgenstein helps us to see that the truth is that *they just happen.*

To get some sense of what justifies speaking of the "myth of mental processes" before we turn to the question of *images,* and eventually most startling of all, the question of *pain,* I will give three or four quotations concerning *thinking, meaning,* and *understanding,* each a word used in a variety of different ways.

Try not to think of understanding as a "mental process" at all. For *that* is the expression which confuses you. . . .

In the sense in which there are processes (including mental processes) which are characteristic

of understanding, understanding is not a mental
process.

(A pain's growing more and less; the hearing of
a tune or sentence, these are mental processes.) (PI
154)

Wittgenstein is saying that the "mental occurrence" (even
if one happened) is not what counts, for the word could
function without it, as it could not function without the
proper circumstances. We might also consider "understanding" used in connection with "understanding a
piece of music or a painting." Even when there is a "sudden click" which we might call a "mental occurrence" the
word "understanding" only applies if what happens after-
wards evinces that this is the right word to use. (A "click"
might be the *wrong* click and have nothing to do with
the matter if the rest of the supporting circumstances
were not there.)

A similar point is made about *thinking*:

While we sometimes call it "thinking" to accom-
pany a sentence by a mental process, that accompaniment is not what we mean by a "thought".——Say
a sentence and think it; say it with understanding.—
And now do not say it, and just do what you accompanied it with when you said it with understanding!
(PI 332)

Some disentangling of usages is going on here. Gaining
greater precision leads to some surprising new insights!

Another common error is aimed at by this:

When I think in language, there aren't "meanings"
going through my mind in addition to the verbal
expressions: the language is itself the vehicle of
thought. (PI 329)

We are trying to find an elusive element that makes thinking meaningful as if it were something added on, as a tune is added to a verse or harmonic embroidery to a melody. But nothing satisfies and nothing short of the complete use itself *could* satisfy.

Sometimes "mental process" seems required to give livingness:

> We want to say "Meaning is surely essentially a mental process, a process of conscious life, not of dead matter." But what will give such a thing the specific character of what goes on?—so long as we think of it as a process. And now it seems to us as if intending could not be any process at all, of any kind whatever.—For what we are dissatisfied with here is the grammar of *process*, not the specific kind of process.—It could be said: we should call any process "dead" in this sense. (Z 236)

It was with regard to *images* that Wittgenstein made the major discovery that came to condition his whole approach to mental events and phenomena. He told a friend that when it first struck him it had almost the force of a revelation: We can never learn anything about images from inspecting our own images, for the *nature of the image is no more and no less than the way the word "image" is used*. It is in this way that we learn, for example, the following:

> The image is not a picture, nor is the visual impression one. Neither "image" nor "impression" is the concept of a picture, although in both cases there is a tie-up with a picture, and a different one in either case. (Z 638)

Suppose I call to mind an image (for images are voluntary

and may be called to mind, and again this is shown by
the way the word is used) of Winston Churchill. I seem
to have in mind then a picture of a short man in a black
coat making a V sign while standing on a sidewalk. I
may even say, "The picture of him on VE-Day comes
back to me." But the grammar of "picture" doesn't work,
for some questions would be quite nonsensical (for
example, Does the picture in your mind *look like him?*).
Images are not compared with what they are images of
in the way that pictures are. *And this we do not find out
from inspecting the images.*

We need to take a step further back and look at the
character of perception itself then. What about the
impression or percept in the mind? How do we recognize phenomena themselves and know what to call
them? In the following passage Wittgenstein formulates
exactly the same problem discussed by Plato in his
Theaetetus, and it arises from the same initial conception
of the human relation to the world. It is the feeling that
perception tells us something about the world prior to
language and that if we had perception alone without
language the world would still have some kind of deter-
minate character. We think of perception (and particularly vision) as a kind of picturing, or at least on the
analogy of picturing. So it seems that something *is there,
and we perceive it apart from words.* This is the way it
seems to be in our own cases as we stare out at familiar
surroundings. Take away the words, and the objects or
sense phenomena would be there unchanged. The corol-
lary is that the mind is furnished with memory traces,
already identified by previous experience which it can
then use to identify subsequent perceptions. This is the
model that gives rise to the *Theaetetus* as well as to
Wittgenstein's remarks:

> Supposing I teach someone the use of the word "yellow" by repeatedly pointing to a yellow patch and pronouncing the word. On another occasion I make him apply what he has learnt by giving him the order, "choose a yellow ball out of this bag". What was it that happened when he obeyed my order? I say "possibly just this: he heard my words and took a yellow ball from the bag". Now you may be inclined to think that this couldn't possibly have been all; and the *kind* of thing that you would suggest is that he imagined something yellow when he *understood* the order and then chose a ball according to his image. To see that this is not *necessary* remember that I could have given him the order, "Imagine a yellow patch." Would you still be inclined to assume that he first imagines a yellow patch, just *understanding* my order, and then imagines a yellow patch to match the first? (BB 11, 12)

The desire for an explanatory intermediary here becomes a *reductio ad absurdum* when it threatens to lead to an infinite regress. Since we will be compelled to accept an immediacy of happening without further linkage somewhere along the line, why not accept it with good grace at the outset? Once we realize that not all language activities can be fitted into the same moulds, Wittgenstein tells us, we will no longer insist that things *must* be a certain way.

Remembering and memory, Wittgenstein reminds us, like perceiving, involve many different ways of speaking. If I am asked, if I remember something, I may answer yes or no without any image coming into my mind at all; or I may say, "I'll try to remember," and screw up my face while various images or words float into my mind, which I more or less direct or do not direct, some seeming to have dates attached and others not. Two of Wittgenstein's closest students, Norman Malcolm and G. E. M. Anscombe, have written most fully on Wittgenstein's conception of memory.3

So far in this book we have dealt with Wittgenstein's abandonment of even the very minimalist metaphysics of his own early philosophy and the resulting new conception of meaning (a step which, as we have indicated, has a parallel in the almost contemporaneous change in Heidegger's philosophy). We then turned to a second, even more innovative, step, the "demetaphysicalizing" of the age-old philosophical-theological "inner world," by which we do not mean, as so many have mistakenly imagined, giving up the "inner life" but rather what could be better described as its "liberation."

This will become clearer as we discuss the topic of what, without the "inner world," happens to the so closely related question of the self. This is where Wittgenstein's discussion of *privacy*, bulking so large in his later philosophy, comes to the fore.

The Illusion of the Private Self

Many have wondered why we do not hear any more about solipsism in Wittgenstein's later philosophy. What happened to the *Tractatus*'s recognition of the truth in such remarks as "All experience is my experience," or "The world is my world"? The answer is that Wittgenstein came to see that solipsism arises from the belief in, or is entirely dependent upon, the conception of the *metaphysically private self.* The solipsistic paradoxes, which we seem compelled to acknowledge and yet obviously cannot accept, all have their source in this conception. The "paradoxes of solipsism" disappear when the closed-off absolutely private metaphysical subject disappears.[4] We do not speak of "my ownership of my own experiences" or "my ownership of myself," though these are the supreme examples of "ownership" and of a kind of ego hegemony, without falling back on the allegedly "logical" principle of self-identity (or self-ownership) with regard to the human self. Self-identity for Wittgenstein was from the start an illusion in any form. To say that "A thing is identical with itself" struck him as an example of saying nothing. In announcing this, both Plato and Aristotle begin their philosophies, as it were, with a kind of *metaphysical imprimatur,* or *initial declaration of the metaphysical position itself.* (The statement "Nothing is self-identical," of course, means nothing either, though it suggests something nearer to the truth of the matter.) When he abandoned self-identity Wittgenstein did not see that both the absolute object and the absolute subject were prescribed in that formula and that solipsism was an inevitable concomitant. The method of clarification of grammar was needed to show the impossibility of an absolutely private language, and hence of an absolutely private self.

We have to be most clear about this because it is the crux of what is most original and most far-reaching in consequences in Wittgenstein's philosophy. Wittgenstein has no animus against privacy. On the contrary, he himself was a very private person. His philosophy, as we have already indicated, may even be said to have arisen out of "inner conversations" with himself. Nor is there any favoring of the social over the individual in his thinking. If anything, his philosophy favors the "cultural" over the "social," or the deeply conventional and traditional over the organizational and the "imposed" from either above or the outside.

To get rid of the metaphysically private self, not to think or experience the world in that way any more, is actually to strike a blow in favor of genuine (i.e., relative) privacy. The former is a *prison*, the latter a *choice*. In the first case the fly is still in the fly-bottle. We might say that real spiritual freedom depends upon giving up the myth that the independence of the self somehow depends upon its having a metaphysical underpinning or valida- tion. The "mystification" lies in the self-identity, not ren- dered any more palatable by Hegel in his coupling of the "in-itself" with the "for-itself." The attempt to ground both self and objects in "in-itselfness" or "own being," in order to guarantee their reality, lies at the very heart of the ratio-mythic "duplication" which created the Metaphysical Age.

We have seen part of the means by which Wittgenstein undoes the way of thinking that locks us into the absolutely private self—that is, his "depsycholo- gizing" of the private "inner world" with its inaccessible (to all but *that* subject) mental processes and objects. The real assault on the metaphysical subject comes with what Wittgenstein students know as the "private lan- guage argument," probably the single most well-known "set piece" in Wittgenstein's later philosophy.

What does this argument consist in?[5] Perhaps we can formulate the upshot of it this way: Wittgenstein was able to establish that even the most primitive language that claims to report a truth can do so only if it has some way of establishing the meaning of its signs independently of the truth it claims to be reporting. No such independent "leverage" exists for an absolutely private language. Therefore, an absolutely private language is a mirage, and so is what goes with it, an absolutely private subject.

(A helpful analogy is a "courtroom" in which both

contesting lawyers and the judge are all one and the same person. Such a "legal" setting would be analogous to the "linguistic" setting in which an imagined absolutely private subject would be ensconced.)

To make the argument we have outlined, Wittgenstein imagines a simple enough case where a human being (it could be any of us) keeps a private diary in which he or she makes a mark every time a certain pain occurs. The "moment of truth" comes when this diarist is unable to fulfill the minimum meaning-requirement of being able to identify, let us say on a particular morning, whether the pain being experienced is the *same* pain as the one she or he has been marking the occurrence of up to that point. His or her own memory cannot independently judge the matter. Therefore, the diary-keeping fails at this point, and with it the possibility of the absolutely private language.

Once again we need to reiterate that, of course, there is nothing wrong with secret codes like those used by Roger Bacon and John Locke (and even, we understand, at one point, Wittgenstein himself). These can easily be created and used. This is not what is at issue. What concerns Wittgenstein is the absolutely private showing of what the language is *about*, the situation that prevents any translation or communication of what the language is supposed to be referring to. We have the impression that the diarist at least can *show himself* what is being referred to, but even this cannot be done because the "identity" of the pain, its sameness, cannot be established by itself. As the philosopher Eric Gutkind put it, "Things do not carry their identity about in themselves." Nothing could be more real than a pain and at the same time nothing could be more inaccessible to anyone, other than the person who "has" it (or, better to say, *is* it). This is fit to be the *pons asinorum,* or Euclid's "fifth postulate," for metaphysics. Euclid's "fifth postulate" proved to be no postulate at all (giving rise to non-Euclidean geometry), and in the same way the "absolutely private self" of capitalism and scientism will also prove to be, and is proved to be by Wittgenstein, an illusion.

Many consequences follow from what on the face of it does not appear such an impressive thought-experiment. Further conclusions can be drawn as the gates close behind us in the strange new country into which we have been propelled: (1) there are no absolutely private objects; (2) there are no absolutely private exhibitions, for example of *pain* or *red* or anything else. Images are not "equivalences." What is pain then? Consider this:

> "Yes, but there is *something* there all the same, accompanying my cry of pain. And it is on account of that that I utter it. And this something is what is important—and frightful."—Only whom are we informing of this? And on what occasion?
>
> Of course, if water boils in a pot, steam comes out of the pot and also pictured steam comes out of the pictured pot. But what if one insisted on saying that there must also be something boiling in the picture of the pot? (PI 296–7)

Now it might seem as if pain is a nothing. But we are deceived by our ability to locate the pain and even describe it to a certain extent to the doctor. Because of this we imagine that it is a genuine private possession. But it is no such thing.

> "But you will surely admit that there is a difference between pain-behaviour accompanied by pain

and pain-behaviour without any pain?"—Admit it? What greater difference could there be?—"And yet you again and again reach the conclusion that the sensation itself is a *nothing*."—Not at all. It is not a *something*, but not a *nothing* either! The conclusion was only that a nothing would serve just as well as a something about which nothing could be said. We have only rejected the grammar which tries to force itself on us here. (PI 304)

We have a tendency to suppose, it seems, that if we can turn our attention upon something, this act itself serves to objectify it, or turn it into a "subjective object." Wittgenstein is calling our attention to the point that this is not so and that there are life-happenings like pain which can only be expressed and *which we do not have an aboutness-relation to*. He points out that in teaching children such words as *pain*, we are not so much giving the child something that the word refers to, like an *apple* or a *pencil*, but teaching it new "pain-behaviour," like a cry or interjection.

The creation of the "inner world" established, as it were, a realm of *spooks* to parallel the realm of absolute objects outside us which we believed *must* be there too, whether, as in the earlier medieval age, they are non-material forms, or, as in the modern scientific age, measurable primary qualities or, as today, forces, fields, or particles. The outer falsified scientistic "objectivism" is paralleled by inner, isolated and locked-away, privatized "subjectivism." These are two sides of an outlook that has to be outgrown *in toto*.

The cultural implications in changing our conception of the self and hence of the individual are bound to be far-reaching indeed. Without the lonely, grasping and fearful, absolutely privatized individual self with which we have lived for so long and which becomes more and more dangerous in our time (because not restrained by any God or objective conscience and more and more convinced that the only reality is power), there is an opportunity at last to give a new meaning to the individualism that is the heart and soul of Christian Europe. The true individual, the only individual who can survive and who deserves to survive, is the inwardly opened individual who has gained not merely civil or political freedom, but spiritual freedom. This is the individual who is open to the Spirit, rather than closed into a falsely conceived Logos. *By transforming the condition of the individual Wittgenstein may well have done more to restore the spiritual health of Europe and the West than all the psychotherapies and economic and technological panaceas it is possible to imagine.*

Wittgenstein's philosophy gives a newer and saner answer to the questions *Who are we?* and *What is a human being?* than we have heard since the days of Socrates. Perhaps it has been worth the thousands of pages of texts and tens of thousands of words that have poured out in our century on these and related subjects to have gained this illumination.

I do not say that we are out of the woods. But I do say that the European individual has been given a new lease on life by Wittgenstein in a way that cannot be gainsaid and may have epochal significance. This change at the heart of our problem may well be the beginning of the opening-up or the "great new prospects" that Wittgenstein said are concealed in his philosophy.

## CHAPTER 7

# Return of
the Ritual

Word language is only one of many possible kinds
of language.

Wittgenstein

In a technological age in which it is believed that all
problems are ultimately of a technical nature, we are
bound to feel that rituals have only minor significance.
They are thought of as window-dressing or, at most, as
ways of promoting social cohesion. We are, effectively,
ritual-blind.

With the loss of the reality of the "inner world" of
mental contents (the "inner facade") there may go a feeling of "inner emptiness," as if the "inner life", which is
freed by this, is no compensation for what is being given
up. And this is where it is important to realize that what
will take the place of the "inner world" as the natural
expression of the "inner life" will be the recovery of the
ritual, that which links us to the ancient pre-metaphysical
ages. The world of the ritual will gain in significance as
the "inner world" disappears.

Ritual and the Inner Life

But we will have to change our thinking about ritual. And this is where Wittgenstein's *Remarks on Frazer's "Golden Bough"* will be of inestimable value. Frazer's book, because it judges ritual as pre-scientific, or based on a false understanding of the world, is an excellent example of one of the prevailing myths of our time, which has blocked off our spiritual perception: the *myth of archaic stupidity*. Everyone in the past, but especially primitive peoples, who did not produce science, is thought of as intellectually inferior. "These people thought that you could make it rain by doing a particular kind of dance." In saying this, we attribute to them the same kind of causal obsession that we have ourselves, as if everything is done to produce results; primitive people were too stupid to see that if they do the dance in the dry season no rain follows, and if they do it at the beginning of the wet season it is bound to rain anyway. We are the ones who are stupid because our understanding is limited to this causal way of thinking.

The situation is similar to some scientistically minded person observing our New Year's Eve parties and remarking: "Look at how foolish these people are; they believe that if they do not make all this noise, the New Year will not come in." Or, watching a ribbon-cutting ceremony at the opening of a new bridge, such a one might remark: "They think that if they do not do this, people will have bad luck on the bridge."

The attempt to "explain" everything, even what does not need any explanation, is a symptom of our "sickness" and produces crude and foolish results when it is extended to primitive customs. Thus, speaking of Frazer, Wittgenstein says:

His explanations of the primitive observances are much cruder than the sense of the observances themselves. (RFGB 8e)

What is the "sense of the observances"? Here Wittgenstein reminds us that we have within us the capacity to understand ancient rituals because the very thing that gave rise to them is still present in us once we get over the idea of "explaining" them. Speaking of the practice of killing the King of the Wood at Nemi in northern Italy, a main theme of Frazer's book, Wittgenstein says:

> The explanation is not what satisfied us anyway. When Frazer begins by telling the story of the King of the Wood at Nemi, he does this in a tone which shows that something strange and terrible is happening here. And that is the answer to the question "Why is this happening?": Because it is terrible. In other words, what strikes us in this course of events as terrible, impressive, horrible, tragic, etc., anything but trivial and insignificant, that is what gave birth to them. (RFGB 3e)

Then he adds:

> Compared with the impression that what is described here makes on us, the explanation is too uncertain.

What grips us in Frazer's story is not his explanation that primitive peoples "see no limit to their power of influencing the course of nature to their own advantage" (*Golden Bough* 11) but rather what we share with them, a sense of the "majesty of death."

Put that account of the King of the Wood at

Nemi together with the phrase "the majesty of death", and you see that they are one.

The life of the priest-king shows what is meant by that phrase.

If someone is gripped by the majesty of death, then through such a life he can give expression to it.—Of course this is not an explanation: it puts one symbol in place of another. Or one ceremony in place of another. (RFGB 3e)

This is the way we understand rituals: by putting one symbol or ceremony familiar to us in place of another not familiar. *Then*, we understand. Consider for example, odd birth or mourning rituals.

Many things may give us a shudder that need no explanation, but simply correspond to a very common human feeling. For example, in the Hapsburg Crypt in the Capuchin Church in Vienna, which Wittgenstein may well have visited as a boy or young man, on one of the tombs is a sculpture of a skull wearing a crown. Again a symbol meaning the same as the "majesty of death." Does this need an "explanation" or to be put in a category of "superstition"? Don't we "understand" very well?

Another feature of ritual is its sometimes reflexivity—for example, the representation of death as itself dead. Wittgenstein sees here a grammatical possibility, something well known in the history of philosophy and in his own philosophy.

To cast out death or slay death; but he is also represented as a skeleton, as in some sense dead himself. "As dead as death". "Nothing is so dead as death, nothing is so beautiful as beauty itself." Here the image which we use in thinking of reality is that beauty, death, etc. are the pure (concentrated) substances, and that they are found in the beautiful object as added ingredients of the mixture.—And do I not recognize here my own observations on "object" and "complex". (RFGB 10e)

We are much closer to primitive peoples in our deeper feelings and instincts than we imagine, and this is not surprising because the framework of human life has not changed.

One could well imagine primitive practices oneself and it would only be by chance if they were not actually to be found somewhere. That is, the principle according to which these practices are ordered is much more general than Frazer shows it to be and we find it in ourselves: we could think out for ourselves the different possibilities. (RFGB 5e)

Of course, this doesn't mean that rituals can just be invented haphazardly. If they are to survive, they have to correspond to something "in our own souls," a "general inclination" we all share.

Frazer misunderstands the primitive response to the world because he sees primitive rituals, not as similar to our own rituals (and arising from a common spirit) and not even as based on a different understanding of the world, but as arising from a false idea of the course of nature.

The nonsense here is that Frazer represents these people as if they had a completely false (even insane) idea of the course of nature, whereas they only possess a peculiar interpretation of the phenomena. That is, if they were to write it down, their knowledge of nature would not differ fundamentally from ours. Only their magic is different. (PO 141)

(It is not clear to me why Wittgenstein says "if they were to write it down," but the difference between firsthand knowledge and "interpretation" is not hard to see.) The kind of contrast between "their magic" and "our magic" implied here has to do not only with our "metaphysics" but also with the kind of *causalism* that we discuss in the next chapter. Finding causes everywhere, even where there are no causes, relates to "our magic."

Rituals, Wittgenstein makes clear, are non-cognitive and non-instrumental. They are not based on opinions and do not aim at anything. *Burning an effigy* or *kissing the picture of a loved one* are not primarily expected to influence events. They do not *aim* at anything. "We act in this way and then feel satisfied."

Recent studies of ritual in relation to performance and theater have brought out a vast range of facets.[1] We can, for example, look at ritual as:

discipline (military, monastic, educational)
spectacle (parades, displays, museums, fashions)
performance (theater, rock groups, sports)
protocol (titles, precedence, celebrities)
life cycles (birthdays, marriages, funerals,
     anniversaries)
daily relations (greetings, gift-giving, family obligations,
     eating)

Perhaps the most important distinction to emerge from these studies is that between *ritual*, which always involves action, and *entertainment*, which contains an element of passivity, or, as the etymology suggests, "interest being mutually held." If we imagine an occasion very typical of today, a Gospel Singing Festival that half the audience sees as a religious service and the other half as an entertainment, we can begin to see the difference, which has to do with how the occasion relates to the rest of life. Culture and religion are often indistinguishable.

Wittgenstein took as a criterion of religious belief the extent to which the whole of life was determined by it or related to it. Would one "go through fire" for it, "summon it up in moments of crisis," etc.? And this is roughly the same kind of difference between the Mass heard in the concert hall and the Mass participated in in the church, or, we might add, the Bible read as "literature" or as "guidance for life." It is not impossible that something of religious significance may be seen in the circus (Kierkegaard and Nietzsche both drew upon circus metaphors for religious illustrations) or in a particular performance of a particular operatic aria, but these will be isolated moments, not integrated into a whole life-pattern, as observing the Sabbath or receiving Communion are.

Rituals of Daily Life

What is most important, however, are the secular rituals of daily life, the traditional prescribed patterns of behavior, which are the most powerful forces in any society. To begin to see this is to begin to understand the weight of Wittgenstein's assertion that "Man is a ceremonial being."

Writing about the *Analects* of Confucius in his book *Confucius—the Secular as Sacred* (N.Y.: Harper, 1972) Herbert Fingarette found the same teaching there: "effortless power coordinating social activity in a civilized community." "With correct comportment, no commands are necessary, yet affairs proceed" (*Analects* 13:6).

> I see you on the street. I smile, walk toward you, put out my hand to shake yours. And behold—

without any command, stratagem, force, special
tricks or tools, without any effort on my part to
make you do so, you spontaneously turn toward
me, return my smile, raise your hand toward mine.
We shake hands,—not by my pulling your hand up
and down or your pulling mine but by spontaneous
and perfect cooperative action. Normally we do not
notice the subtlety and amazing complexity of this
coordinated "ritual" act. (Fingarette 9)

Such actions depend upon attitudes of mutual
respect, as well as upon learned and accepted conventions. There is an element of the *magical* involved
because, as with all "performatives," great effects are produced effortlessly; once the initial gesture has been made
in the proper ceremonial context, "from there onward
everything 'happens'." Human life is full of words that
function in this ritual way,—*I promise, I agree, I can't
make it*—where the words themselves *are* the acts. The
mutual respect involved is not the same as a conscious
feeling of mutual respect, Fingarette points out; "it is fully
expressed in the correct, 'live' and spontaneous performance of the act." The implications are far-reaching.

What we have come to see, in our own way, is how
vast is the area of human existence in which the
substance of that existence *is* the ceremony.
Promises, commitments, excuses, pleas, compli-
ments, pacts—these and so much more are ceremonies or they are nothing. It is thus in the medium
of ceremony that the peculiarly human part of our
life is lived. The ceremonial act is the primary irre-
ducible event; language cannot be understood in
isolation from the conventional practice in which it

is rooted; conventional practice cannot be understood in isolation from the language that defines and
is part of it. (Fingarette 14)

The idea of a "universalistic community based upon
shared conventions," which Fingarette finds in Confucius,
is especially compatible to Wittgenstein because this is
essentially his understanding of the nature of mathematics, once its residual metaphysical baggage has been discarded. The Confucian idea of the "rectification of the
names"—that is, restoring to words their proper weights
and meanings—might, without too much effort, be
shown to be entirely compatible with the deep grammar
of ordinary language, as that is connected with the natural norms of ordinary life.[2]

In the Confucian world the person of *jen* (true
humanness) is the one who carries out in a sacred way *li*
(the daily social patterns of conduct and relationship).
Confucius

saw how miraculous a power, how humane a power
was inherent in well-learned conventional practices
as distinguished from force, threats, and commands.
Finally he saw that the dignity peculiar to man and
the power associated with this dignity could be
characterized in terms of holy rite, of ceremony. For
ceremony is a conventionalized practice in which
are emphasized intrinsic harmony, beauty and
sacredness. (Fingarette 63)

The ideas of trying to impose rituals by force or of
repeating dead rituals mechanically after the life and
beauty have gone out of them are so at odds with the
Confucian understanding of *li* and *jen* that these matters
are not even discussed in the *Analects*.

Wittgenstein is very aware of ritual gone dead or connected with force. Hence statements like these:

> Everything ritualistic (everything that, as it were, smacks of the high priest) must be strictly avoided, because it immediately turns rotten.
>
> Of course a kiss is a ritual too, and it isn't rotten, but ritual is permissible only to the extent that it is as genuine as a kiss. (CV 8e)

The "high priestly" sense, which suggests compulsion, is the opposite of deep responses coming from the human soul in well-loved ceremonies or in gestures like the sincere kiss. In his Foreword to *Philosophical Remarks*, Wittgenstein expresses his aversion to ritual expressions that would not be understood today and would be "chicanery" if used.

> I would like to say "This book is written to the glory of God", but nowadays that would be chicanery, that is, it would not be rightly understood. (PR 7)

In an intellectual environment like ours today the ritual phrase that occurred to Wittgenstein as a possible dedication cannot but appear to others as fraudulent. By comparison, the daily ritual of the kiss, however sometimes perfunctory, remains a living symbol. Or waving goodbye. But "God" does not function so.

If "universality" and "humanness" are part of the nature of true ritual, this might well serve as a basis for criticizing other rituals (particular those connected with war and human sacrifice). But this is not followed up by either Wittgenstein or Confucius.

## CHAPTER 8

Redemption of Action

Action is without a way.
It *is* the Way.
Eric Gutkind

When we look at the spiritual impact of Wittgenstein's philosophy, particularly for the future, two things stand out. The first is coming to the end of the inner world of "mental contents" (inner "dialogical thinking" replaces "inner knowing"). The second is disentangling human action from the bewitchment of causality. One of the main effects of scientism and technologism, as dominant ways of thinking in our age, has been to make us see "causes" everywhere, treating human action as if it were a form of causality, hypostatizing psychological and social "forces" as if they were "causal agents" (this being itself a hybrid mythic notion).

It is, to begin with, important to draw a line between *behavior* and *action*, which is also the line between *cause* and *reason*. This is the first step toward recovering the immediacy, autonomy, and uniqueness of action, as over against all causality.[1]

Grammar and Action

The nature of action is such that it resists causal explanation, not because of metaphysical differences but because of categorical or grammatical ones. If we take a simple case of body movement, let us say *I decide to put up my hand* during the question period after a lecture. Was my *decision* or my *will* the *cause* of my hand going up? Or was *I* the *cause?* No, I was the *agent.* I decided, and the hand went up without anything "in between." Like all acts, this one had "no volume" as Wittgenstein would say, no connecting links.

We sometimes imagine *willing* itself as the *cause* of our voluntary actions. Wittgenstein discusses this at some length (PI 611–629). He says that willing is not the name of an action; it is not something that we do or bring about. Nor is it the name of a mental event, a phenomenon or an experience. In other words, if I raise my arm voluntarily, there is not something in between me and my action that could be identified as the "willing." My arm "just goes up." Or, as he says:

> *Doing* itself seems not to have any volume of experience. It seems like an extensionless point, the point of a needle. This point seems to be the real agent. And the phenomenal happenings only to be consequences of this acting. "I *do* . . ." seems to have a definite sense separate from all experience. (PI 620)

Over and over again we see that there is no "machinery of action," no "how-to." No how-to raise your arm, open your mouth, or shake your head. Complicated movements require practice; simple ones do not. Even learned gestures, done apparently by imitation, have no "how-to."

If somebody asks me, "Why did you put your hand up?" they are asking me to give a *reason* not a *cause*. I might reply: "Because I thought it was the question period," or "I just *had* to question something he said" or "I wanted to get my question in before Professor So-and-So's." (These are not causal reports, which might rather go like this: "I have observed myself on many occasions and I have noticed that I tend to put my hand up after lectures." Cause is an *observation* term. Action is not "caused.")

The distinction between *reasons* and *causes* has to be made clear because it becomes critical when we come to questions about motives or desires or impulses; here the temptation to turn reasons into causes becomes particularly strong. Roughly speaking, reasons are what we learn from the person doing the action; they answer the question *why?* by reporting a particular way the person doing the action has gone, a justification for doing or saying something. Causes, on the other hand, are observation terms, reporting relations between phenomena on the basis of evidence, experiment, conjecture, hypothesis. Wittgenstein sums up the difference:

> In a law-court you are asked the motive of your action and you are supposed to know it. . . . You are not supposed to know the laws by which your body and mind are governed. (LC 21)

Other people can, of course, guess your motives or question them or reject them, as they can guess, question, or reject your reasons. The grammar here is quite different from the grammar of cause and effect. People are not supposed to know what *caused* their behavior but are supposed to know what their *reasons* for acting were.

How these two kinds of grammar get mixed together

may be illustrated by a sentence like "The sound made me jump." The first thing to observe is that the sound didn't *do* anything; there was an event followed by another event, which I report in a way that may be misleading. The notion that the sound *did* something arises from mixing it with my *reason* for jumping (there could conceivably have been another reason) because sound *is* a well-known *cause* for people jumping. And now it looks as if the sound was a causal agent even though there are no causal agents. The mistake is a confusion of language.

Suppose I am asked, "Why are you so afraid?" and I reply, "It is because that man made threatening gestures." Here I have a reason and (very likely) the man has a reason. The causal connection is also well known. The form of the question still asks for a reason and still has a different sense from a question that might be answered by someone else saying, "He has just been given a certain drug which produces a fear response."

There are two kinds of answers to many questions even when the form of the questions makes it look as if both answers are of the same kind. If somebody asks, "What was the cause of your injuries?" and you reply, "An automobile accident," and then they ask, "What was the cause of the accident?" and you reply, "Carelessness," the second question and answer clearly report something of a different character from the first. The first is in the realm of *public observation*, the second in that of *first-person testimony*.

"The wind blew the chimney down" and "The man pulled the chimney down." Here the result is the same, and we know that the wind, if it reaches a certain velocity, may indeed blow chimneys down, while there may be many reasons why a man would pull a chimney down. The wind is not an agent; the man is. If we say "the man caused" the result, his action is still not merely of a casual kind. Because it was an act, there is more to find out about it, which doesn't fall in the category of repeated observation.

Motives, desires, wishes, beliefs, intentions are not causes, but reasons. This is a grammatical statement. Of all of them can be asked what Wittgenstein asks about causes and motives:

> What is the difference between cause and motive?— How is the motive discovered and how the cause? (PI 224)

What kind of questions do we ask and of whom do we ask them? Different language-games are played with different words. And in different contexts the same answers may have very different meanings.

In the case of strong emotions or irresistible impulses or compulsions, a person may give as a reason for doing something that he or she was overpowered, as if in the grip of an agency other than themselves. The statement "I couldn't help myself" also gives a reason, even if intended to deny responsibility, and it may still be contrasted with statements like "He always says such things when he gets angry." In this latter case we may be noting a symptom.

This brings us to the question of *justification*, a blanket term that covers *reasons* we give for our action and wants, and also *criteria*, the means by which we identify phenomena or complexes of phenomena. We have to examine the grammar of the word *justify* and the language-games in which it functions.[2]

The most important point about justification is that it has to appeal to "something independent." We cannot justify ourselves to ourselves or only in imagination.

Let us imagine a table (something like a dictionary) that exists only in our imagination. A dictionary can be used to justify the translation of a word X by a word Y. But are we also to call it a justification if such a table is to be looked up only in the imagination?—"Well, yes; then it is a subjective justification."—But justification consists in appealing to something independent.—"But surely I can appeal from one memory to another. For example, I don't know if I have remembered the time of departure of a train right and to check it I call to mind how a page of the time-table looked. Isn't it the same here?"—No; for this process has got to produce a memory which is actually *correct*. If the mental image of the time-table could not itself be *tested* for correctness, how could it confirm the correctness of the first memory? (As if someone were to buy several copies of the morning paper to assure himself that what it said was true.) (PI 265)

The point here parallels that with regard to the impossibility of a private language. "Why can't my left hand give my right hand money?" asks Wittgenstein. It is for the same reason that I cannot justify the choice of dimensions for a bridge only in imagination. The hands of the clock are fastened to the dial, which now revolves carrying the hands with it. So we play games with ourselves.

For if I need a justification for using a word, it must also be one for someone else. (PI 378)

Justifications can be good or bad, just as there can be good dictionaries and bad dictionaries, good reasons and bad reasons, accurate records and inaccurate records. Wittgenstein is making the point that to *feel* justified or to *imagine* that one is justified is not the same thing as to *be* justified, however adequate or inadequate this may be. Self-justification is no justification at all, any more than a person in a court can sit as judge in his own case. It seems obvious, but much turns on it.

Justifications, like reasons, have to be accepted by other people. They have a conventional aspect.

> What people accept as a justification—is shewn by how they think and live. (PI 325)

We can imagine special cases, some perhaps depicted in literature, in which a person, having been universally condemned, nevertheless maintains his or her innocence, believing in vindication by evidence. Justification in the eyes of others is what is sought.

Justification in more ordinary cases, Wittgenstein points out, may appeal to experience, tradition, success, or to knowledge, theories, beliefs. All these in turn may need to be justified. But it is the character of justification, Wittgenstein says, that it *come to an end*. Grammar, language-games, and forms of life do not need to be justified and cannot be. They are "given." If, for example, under normal circumstances we teach a child arithmetic, this doesn't need to be justified. And if the child asks for reasons for the calculations being just the way they are, the reply is:

> Somewhere we must be finished with justification, and then there remains the proposition that *this* is how we calculate. (OC 212)

The certainty involved here is not impaired by the possibility that we *could* do it some other way (OC 375, 498). Of the kind of certainty involved in language-games Wittgenstein says:

> I want to conceive it as something that lies beyond
> being justified or unjustified; as it were, as some-
> thing animal. (OC 359)

Knowing and Certainty

Toward the end of his life, in his last book, which
came to be called *On Certainty*, Wittgenstein wrote that
certain empirical propositions (such as being able to
identify parts of my body or ordinary objects or my own
name) "seem to underlie all questions and all thinking,
though this is not a matter of knowing" (OC 414, 415).
He speaks of the "entire system of our language-games"
and of its "foundations" (OC 411).

> If I say "*we assume* that the earth has existed for
> many years past" (or something similar), then of
> course it sounds strange that we should *assume* such
> a thing. But in the entire system of our language-
> games it belongs to the foundations. The assump-
> tion, one might say, forms the basis of action, and,
> therefore, naturally, of thought. (OC 411)

It is surprising to find both the words *system* and *foundations* being used in connection with all language-games.
In the *Philosophical Investigations*, *system* is only applied
to certain specific language-games which have that character, and *Fundament* is used only twice (PI 87, 89), in
connections that have nothing to do with language-games.

Students have had great difficulty identifying what
these last notes are all about. As so often happens with
Wittgenstein, we understand, or think we do, what he is
saying but don't get the point of it. Why does it matter to
him so much? And this is the case with *On Certainty*,
which has a clear enough theme, whose importance

seems to elude us. Is he looking for *absolute* certainty?

The theme of *On Certainty* is G. E. Moore's pointing to a tree and saying, "This tree exists," or, "I know this is a tree." He is looking for absolute intellectual certainty. And this, Wittgenstein says, is not the kind of certainty we need or can have. Wittgenstein's view is that such statements make sense if they occur in specific language-games, if they answer specific questions or genuine doubts, but do not make sense as said by the traditional philosopher like Moore with no setting at all. But this distinction is only the *beginning* of the problem in *On Certainty*, because what we really want to know is why is Moore compelled to say what he does and what is really bothering him? Moore, it might seem, wants a particular kind of certainty (a super-certainty or epistemic certainty or metaphysical certainty), which may not be available; but still he may not be convinced it is not unless the whole matter is described more clearly than it has been so far. The following two remarks may lead us into this deeper problem:

> Someone might ask me: "How certain are you that that is a tree over there, that you have money in your pocket, that that is your foot?" And the answer in one case might be "not certain", in another "as good as certain", in the third "I can't doubt it". And these answers would make sense even without any grounds. I should not need, for example, to say: "I can't be certain whether that is a tree because my eyes aren't sharp enough". I want to say it made sense for Moore to say "I *know* that this is a tree", if he meant something quite particular by it.
>
> (I believe it might interest a philosopher, one who can think himself, to read my notes. For even if

> I have hit the mark only rarely, he would recognize
> what targets I have been ceaselessly aiming at.) (OC
> 387)

Now "what targets," especially in this case, has
Wittgenstein been "ceaselessly aiming at"? A few pages
later we will find the answer, however little we are able
to make of it:

> What I am aiming at is also found in the differ-
> ence between the casual observation "I know that
> that's a . . .", as it might be used in ordinary life, and
> the same utterance when a philosopher makes it.
> (OC 406)

Why does this matter so much? It is obviously because of
the enormous philosophical implications of Moore's
attempt to "prove the existence of an external world" by,
for example, holding up his hand, staring at it and saying, "This is a hand." (Or the same thing with a tree.) It is
not so easy to describe exactly what is wrong here. And
this is what Wittgenstein tells us in this note:

> But is it an adequate answer to the scepticism
> of the idealist, or the assurances of the realist, to say
> that "There are physical objects" is nonsense? For
> them after all it is not nonsense. It would, however,
> be an answer to say: this assertion, or its opposite is
> a misfiring attempt to express what can't be
> expressed like that: And that it does misfire can be
> shewn; but that isn't the end of the matter. We need
> to realize that what presents itself to us as the first
> expression of a difficulty, or of its solution, may as
> yet not be correctly expressed at all. Just as one who
> has a just censure of a picture to make will often at
> first offer the censure where it does not belong, and

> an *investigation* is needed in order to find the right point of attack for the critic. (OC 37)

Wittgenstein comes at the same problem again and again to bring out the difference between what *he* wants to say and what *Moore* wants to say. Where Moore would like to raise doubts where no doubts seem possible—e.g., Does that tree really exist or not?—when everyone can see it clearly, Wittgenstein would simply say to him, "Rubbish." But if Moore went on, in the manner of a philosopher, to say, "I *know* that it does," Wittgenstein would feel that now he needs to be corrected (OC 498). Using the supercharged word *know* outside of all normal contexts makes it no longer seem to be saying anything, and becomes "philosophically astonishing" (OC 622).

The difference between what Moore wants to say and what Wittgenstein wants to say comes down to something deceptively simple:

> I should like to say: Moore does not *know* what he asserts he knows, but it stands fast for him, as also for me; regarding it as absolutely solid is part of our *method* of doubt and enquiry. (OC 151)

He compares this to the axis around which a body rotates. Nothing holds the axis fast, "but the movement around it determines its immobility."

> No one ever taught me that my hands don't disappear when I am not paying attention to them. Nor can I be said to presuppose the truth of this proposition in my assertions etc. (as if they rested on it) while it only gets sense from the rest of our procedure of asserting. (OC 153)

We cannot be mistaken about the general human judgments that determine what a mistake is without being regarded as *demented* (OC 155). (That would have happened if Moore, looking at a tree had said: This is *not* a tree.) It even begins to look as if the philosopher has something in common with the mentally ill because he is asking such bizarre questions.

Intruding the word "know" on the normalcy that "stands fast" lends that normalcy no greater certainty but only a spurious *impression* of greater certainty. Existent otherness (the "external world") is not given as something we can or need to *know* in this peculiar way, but only as part of the normal setting for human life in its stability, regularity and continuing recognizability. (And the rest is a dream.) The fact that this normalcy can, as it were, in a flash disappear—through insanity (OC 217, 281, 419, 572, 674), drugs (OC 676), delusions (OC 624), mental disturbances (OC 71), unheard-of happenings (OC 517), bewilderment and confusion (OC 304, 420), blindness (OC 418) or what we call "awakening" (OC 578, 645)—in no way calls into question its sufficient certainty. We cannot doubt it because neither "doubt" nor "knowing" make sense except in terms of it. Human normality is the native setting within which doubting and knowing take place, and it is "presumptuous" to try to justify or give reasons for the setting (OC 553). There is no certainty that can hold beyond normal life.

The picture of the world that I have is the "inherited background against which I distinguish between true and false." And Wittgenstein continues:

> The propositions describing this world-picture might be part of a kind of mythology. And their role is like that of rules of a game; and the game is

learned purely practically, without learning any explicit rules.

It might be imagined that some propositions, of the form of empirical propositions, were hardened and functioned as channels for such empirical propositions as were not hardened but fluid; and that this relation altered with time, in that fluid propositions hardened, and hard ones became fluid.

The mythology may change back into a state of flux, the riverbed of thoughts may shift. But I distinguish between the movement of waters on the riverbed and the shift of the bed itself; though there is not a sharp division of the one from the other. (OC 95–97)

We see from this that Wittgenstein wants to transform the empty epistemological "ceremony" of "knowing" the "own being" of objects by-fixing-attention-on-them-*as-other*, into an acceptance of a natural human milieu, leaving the transcendent for the ethical and the supernatural. The attempt to get at the phenomena "dehumanized" or "transcendentalized" turns out to "misfire" when the activities of "doubting" and "knowing" are seen to be illusory in their supposed contextless role. Wittgenstein's view is that the certainties of normal human life do not need to be further justified and that in trusting them we make no mistakes, for they define what "mistakes" are, just as they define what "knowing" and "doubting" are. If all these certainties were to give way, it would not make them any the less certain, for the imagined viewpoint from which they would not be certain is not our viewpoint (or indeed even God's); it has no reality at all.

There is a definite resemblance between Wittgenstein's argument against super or metaphysical "knowing" of the externality of objects and his argument against the inner "knowing" of private images and pains. In each case there is a familiar frame of mind: the feeling that we can establish a criterion of identity by fixing our attention in a peculiar way either on the inner object, which I call *mine* in some transcendental sense, or on the outer object, which I call not-mine, also in some transcendental sense. Wittgenstein's examinations reveal that in each case we are engaged in an imaginary "knowing." We can see why he says that the word *know* does not "tolerate a metaphysical emphasis" (OC 482, Cf. OC 260, 435) though the word has been at the center of such emphasis for 2,000 years.

Living in a time when *ideological certitudes* seem willing to risk the destruction of the world and when there is a recrudescence of equally divisive *fundamentalist certitudes*, we are ready for Wittgenstein's profound questioning of traditional *metaphysical certitude*. Such is the historical source for the scientistic certitude of our age, now the unwitting ally of these other super-certitudes. They are *all* illusions.

It is in this context that Wittgenstein's conception of *natural* or *ordinary certainty* should be considered. His understanding that we cannot attain, through supposed "metaphysical knowing," to a greater degree of certainty than the natural normal human certainties of daily life undercuts the super-certitude of science, as well as its mimicking passionate ideological counterparts. Even science in this respect functions as a kind of security blanket.

Knowing and *certainty* belong to different categories and worlds. We might imagine that by linking them together, as in traditional philosophy and as more recent-ly in Cartesianism and the philosophy of the Enlightenment, we are protected against the fevers of fanaticism and power and group ego. But scientistic certainty is already divorced from human practice and relations, and this is a gap that ideologies and fundamentalisms are only too available to fill. Atomic physics (praised for its "technical sweetness" by the developer of the atomic bomb), by claiming an ethical neutrality for its absolutistic pretensions, invited passionate pseudo-scientific myths to supply the practical historical and political content and direction which the cult of "pure science" had opened the way for. (Hence it was not unusual to find theoretical physicists who were also Communists or Fascists or their willing abettors. Scientism offered no protection at the human level against such atrocities, in which indeed it played a part, as the Holocaust, Hiroshima, Nagasaki and Dresden.)

Natural or ordinary certainty, as Wittgenstein understands it, is an "action" category, something that belongs to the way we normally act and normally think, and that needs no further justification or reason. We take for granted the normal stabilities of our lives, even in the midst of earth-shaking catastrophes. (And of what use but cold comfort would other types of certainty be?) In the midst of hell we go on believing that it is not "normal" and that the normal will someday return. In that situation we might be willing to trade all ideologies, beliefs, and commitments for a return to the everyday certainties which, perhaps because we did not understand them and value them in the right way, we permitted to be destroyed.

CHAPTER 9

Entering
an Unknown
Country

The aspects of things that are most important to us are hidden because of their very simplicity and familiarity.

Wittgenstein

In the course of our discussion we have seen Wittgenstein's philosophy bringing into question the whole inner realm of mental phenomena and mental processes (not to question the value of such concepts as *thinking, understanding* and *knowing,* but to dislodge the pictures that we have for so long attached to them). We have also seen him objecting to the causal kind of "explaining," which spreads everywhere, above all interfering with a clear understanding of the nature of human action. As with the "inner world," something interferes with the immediacy and clarity of thinking and acting. And we have also seen Wittgenstein's attempt to free the surety of natural action, the trust and certainty of ordinary everyday life, from the claims to super-certainties provided by modern science and modern ideologies.

A further word is in order about the demoniacal world of modern ideologies in which psychological and social "forces" are imagined not as "causes" in scientific hypotheses (though the causal appearance is maintained), but as agents that control human behavior. These mythical systems, eliciting passionate semi-religious belief, while at the same time maintaining a veneer of science, have unleashed into the world "class," "race" and "unconscious complexes" as godlike realities which we try to get on the good side of, though they are, after all, just abstractions. Wittgenstein's defense of natural certainties as entirely sufficient certainty, like his establishing of the autonomy and uniqueness of human action as against all causal interference and presumed superior "explanations," is an appeal to sanity in the midst of various types of madness.

But it is more than that because it also introduces a new sense of wonder into the everyday, a place where we might least perhaps expect to find it. Many writers have commented on the way in which Wittgenstein's philosophy reveals strangeness in the ordinary and the commonplace. Looking very closely at things that we have taken for granted for so long that they no longer amaze us, Wittgenstein has succeeded in seeing them afresh. What is most obvious, suddenly under his gaze becomes what we have never realized it was before, enigmatic.

This is the liberating effect of Wittgenstein's philosophy. We may easily imagine that it is similar to the effect produced by other great philosophers in the past, who also opened up new worlds. We have only to think of the effects on their own and immediately successive generations of Descartes, Berkeley, Kant and Hegel, to mention only a few. And, of course, the excitement has by no means disappeared. A whole new world is opened up.

The Mystery of the Ordinary

Wittgenstein himself described what he was exploring as an "unknown country." It could not be explored in a straight line but only by many crisscrossing trips, traversing the same places from different sides. (He once compared himself to a tour bus guide who brought people back to the same boulevards from different directions to give them a better familiarity with a city.)

We are not, on the other hand, interested in the unknown country, *in toto*. (Wittgenstein in his later philosophy has no "philosophical system.") What we are investigating are "dark spots" or "confused spots" in the unknown territory, i.e. philosophical problems. Wittgenstein's interest is, and remains, philosophy, which means he is concerned with language as possibilities, not as facts. Where there are many interconnecting difficulties (as with the word *know* discussed in the last chapter), we have something like crucial mountain passes or continental watersheds in the terrain.

This metaphor stresses the unfamiliarity of the country Wittgenstein takes us into. But what is most surprising is the reversal of faces this entails. It is just what we took to be the most familiar and well-established matter-of-fact realities that were revealed to be the unknown country. No new theories, facts or opinions were put forward. We are simply looking at the familiar ordinary world in a new way, and it turns out to be *terra incognita*.

How did Wittgenstein perform this remarkable transformation? In his own personal Notebooks he mentions two practices in his thinking which we should note:

(1) put the question deep down (CV 62, 74);
(2) pray for insight into what lies in front of everyone's eyes (CV 6).

Both of these may be summed up in another injunction:

(3) where others go on ahead, I stay in one place (he might have added "and look") (CV 66)

What we learn from Wittgenstein is that if we look with the greatest intensity at what is most obvious, suddenly it is no longer obvious at all. We could presumably have learned from the religions that the greatest mysteries are hidden in what is closest at hand, but, of course, these are just words if we are preoccupied with the anxieties of life. Wittgenstein's ability to *stand still* argues a special gift at a time when everybody is on the move. Those who are running cannot think deeply about another direction.

"There is no place to go. We are already where we ought to be." These words, paraphrased from the 1930 Notebooks, might be put at the head of all of Wittgenstein's writings, especially after he had thrown away the ladder mentioned in the *Tractatus* (6.54) and even given it up as an auxiliary device, declaring that he was no longer interested in any place that could be reached by a ladder (CV 7e). Wittgenstein keeps aiming at the same targets, the same spots, inexhaustibly, as if success were always imminent. Years did indeed pass before certain clues were deciphered.

Just as important as Wittgenstein's gifts as a thinker was the historical moment in which he lived. It was the moment when language was emerging into philosophical consciousness, coming to the center of the stage in the form of the problem of meaning. It was in this moment that Heidegger (much helped by Husserl as well as by his studies of Duns Scotus) raised the question of the "meaning of Being," while Wittgenstein (much influenced by Gottlob Frege) focused on the "meaning of propositions" (i.e. language).

In hindsight, what we can see is that both these philosophers were moving toward carrying through the "language revolution," even to the point where language would, as it were, supersede metaphysics. The end point in each case was the priority of language (and for Heidegger we would have to add "and thinking") to both object and subject, Being and *Dasein*. Language, we might say, is where they meet and where they were born, for they are, after all, words. We will leave the discussion of Heidegger to others and simply note what this means in the case of Wittgenstein.

What Wittgenstein was getting at was that language is the essence of things. (He called it the "shadow of possibilities thrown on things," though he might well have preferred the word *aspect* even more.) Nothing can come before language; there is nothing "given" before it. Language, as it were, "surrounds" both objects-and-subjects, world-and-human, body-and-mind. But if language is the essence of these, what is the essence of language? Wittgenstein's first shot (*Tractatus*) was: analytic presuppositions of pure logic, i.e., formal structures common to both propositions and facts, defining a total ultimate realm of meaning-possibilities. This left, as a minimal self-denying metaphysics, abstracted to an almost vanishing ideality: absolute subjects (as point-co-ordinates for sense qualities in different property spaces) and the "metaphysical subject" as a point without content at the limit of the world (T 5.632, 5.633, 5.6331). This metaphysics is so attenuated that it is ready to give way altogether, and it did.

The second shot (*Philosophical Investigations*) was: the grammar of ordinary language, the ways we commonly use even philosophical words when we are not misled or confused by metaphysical expressions. There is no more talk of isomorphic combinatorial point-structures. The philosophical super-words that seemed to require this type of analysis have all been returned to their home ports, where their everyday usage turns out to be quite sufficient to do away with even the need or temptation to inflate their significance by ideal abstraction.

If we think of language in its ordinary possibilities of meaning (that aspect of it) as what replaces metaphysics, this may sound too much like the *Tractatus* (the ladder that has to be thrown away). Metaphysics doesn't need to have anything "replace" it. When it is really gone there won't be a sense of *anything taking its place.* We might say that we have never really yet lived in the ordinary world, but this only says that it was demeaned by being compared to something more fundamental or real, in the way that people today may think of the scientific world of physics as somehow more real than the ordinary human world, and indeed it does change the ordinary world.

Having spent hundreds of years thinking of language as an "intermediary" between subject and object, human and world (the "metaphysical stance"), we will not easily upset this to take ordinary language as the natural norm rather than as a new metaphysical foundation. That is why we need the actual method of seeing how the metaphysical temptations and difficulties disappear when looked at in this new way.

Nothing gives grammar the status of logical necessity or any reason or justification beyond itself. It embodies conventional rules that, as root human norms, cannot be "explained." This freedom and autonomy of the essential aspect of language Wittgenstein underlines thus:

> Grammar is not accountable to any reality. It is grammatical rules that determine meaning (constitute

it) and so they themselves are not answerable to any meaning and to that extent are arbitrary. (PG 184)

He compares this with "cookery rules," which he says are not arbitrary because the concept of "cookery" is defined by the "end of cookery," while the concept of "language" is not defined by the end of language, for there is no one end of language. Language remains its own standard and its own master.

Wittgenstein is no longer bothered by an "objectivity" that lies outside of all language, culture and human norms, one that is supposed to set the standard for all truth and meaning. Objectivity is now a product of human agreements in language and action. (If we persist in thinking that in this account "something is missing," it may be because we have not yet caught a glimpse of the sufficiency, completeness, and ungroundedness of sense-making language.)

The *Tractatus* world is a world of facts, and the only kind of language that makes real sense is the language that represents facts. All values are nowhere in the world, but only outside it. (We note that Wittgenstein talked about the world as a whole, that is, as one self-contained system, a way of thinking itself developed in modern science and logic. This is where *logicism* (the idealization of analytic logic), allied with scientism, has brought us. Facts and values could not be more sharply separated, and it seemed as if language itself was not fit to express anything else. How did we get into such a hole? We will look at this question in the next chapter. For now the point is to see that Wittgenstein did get out of it and that he came to understand language, meaning, and grammar as being as multifarious, wide-ranging and surprising as ordinary life itself.

What will interest philosophers especially is the way facts and values mingle together as they do in ordinary life. This is what we mean by speaking of the *normative* character of Wittgenstein's conception of language, meaning, and grammar. This does not mean that language cannot be looked at as *fact* (linguistics) or *physiognomy* (style, "appearances"). But it can also be looked at as *rule* or *custom*, which is to say *normatively*. We refer back to our discussion of "Dimensions of Meaning" in Chapter 5, where these four aspects were outlined, together with grammar as *possibility*. A look at the way the words *rule* and *custom* function will show what is meant by calling them normative. Except in special circumstances we do not call *rules* and *customs* "correct," because they are what determine correctness. Rules and customs are continually undergoing changes for many reasons, but while they are in effect they function as norms that control or guide behavior. Obeying-a-rule or following-a-custom should not be thought of initially as facts. This is not how they are to be taken, any more than the sign *Roller-Skating Prohibited* at the entrance to the park has the same kind of meaning as *Roller-Skating Convention.* Language itself has a normative aspect because it has inbuilt standards of intelligibility that cannot be understood factually. We have to be able to follow rules "blindly" to learn language-games, as well as pronunciation, word-choice and syntax.

What is Thinking?

In Wittgenstein's philosophic work, which is "to bring words back from their metaphysical to their everyday use" (PI 116), possibly no word is more important and tests his method of grammatical and conceptual

clarification better than the word *thinking*. It is discussed
at length in the *Investigations* (316–362), *Zettel* (88–153)
and *Philosophical Grammar* (62–68). In addition there
are references to Wittgenstein's own practice from his
Notebooks in *Culture and Value*, for example, his distinction between "thoughts which occur deep down and
thoughts which bustle about on the surface" (CV 42e),
and his reference to "the thought working its way
towards the light" (CV 47e), and what is needed for philosophizing: "When you are philosophizing you have to
descend into primeval chaos and feel at home there" (CV
65e). These *thoughts about thoughts* should always in the
case of Wittgenstein be put in this context:

> If you want to go down deep you do not need
> to travel far; indeed you don't have to leave your
> most immediate and familiar surroundings. (CV 50e)

As we might expect, Wittgenstein emphasizes the
many different ways in which the concept of *thinking* is
used.

> "Thinking", a widely ramified concept. A con-
> cept that comprises many manifestations of life. The
> phenomena of thinking are widely scattered. (Z 110)
> It is not to be expected of this word that it
> should have a unified employment; we should
> rather expect the opposite. (Z 112)

We can imagine many different things to which the word
thinking is applied. The picture or model that seems
most pervasive is that of thinking as an accompaniment
of speaking or acting.

> The concept "thinking" is formed on the model
> of a kind of imaginary auxiliary activity. (Z 106)
> The boundary-line that is drawn here between

> "thinking" and "not thinking" would run between
> two conditions which are not distinguished by any-
> thing in the least resembling a play of images. (For
> the play of images is admittedly the model according
> to which one would like to think of thinking.) (Z 94)

Wittgenstein is emphatic that thinking is not an *accompaniment* of speaking or doing, just as "expressiveness"
in playing the piano is not something added on to ordinary playing. Nor do we get anywhere by trying to
observe and report what goes on *in us* when we think.
This is practically never of interest.

> Isn't it the same here as with a calculating prodi-
> gy?—He has calculated right if he has got the right
> answer. Perhaps he himself cannot say what went on
> in him. And if we were to hear it, it would perhaps
> seem like a queer caricature of calculation. (Z 89)

It is sometimes important to distinguish between actions
carried out mechanically and actions carried out thought-
fully. But this distinction cannot be made in terms of different experiences. We would have to look into the
grammar of an expression such as "paying attention."

Wittgenstein was much interested in the connection
between "thinking" and "talking to oneself." And I think
we will see why if we consider what is perhaps the single most personally revealing sentence he ever wrote
about his own philosophical method:

> Nearly all my writings are private conversations with
> myself. Things that I say to myself tête-à-tête. (CV
> 77e)[1].

It is very interesting that this entry is immediately followed by "Ambition is the death of thought," which I
take to be a suggestion that the "private conversations"

cannot be carried on in a spirit of ambition. Ambition shuts them off.

It is against the background of this entry that we should consider a curious detail, what to my knowledge may be the only occasion Wittgenstein asked his translator and editor to make a correction in the finished text. Elizabeth Anscombe inserted a footnote, later withdrawn in the first American edition of the *Philosophical Investigations*, after the last sentence of paragraph 32 which read, "And 'think' would here mean something like 'talk to itself'." The footnote read:

> Wittgenstein later rejected this. See e.g. p. 217. He asked me to make such a note. G.E.M.A.

We have here, in a tiny compass, an excellent illustration of the Wittgenstein method. He had apparently been struck by the similarity between one meaning of the word "thinking" and "talking to oneself," and uncharacteristically failed to note that these concepts are also very different. There are many times when "talking to ourselves" has nothing to do with "thinking." In fact, on page 217 of PI he puts it even more strongly:

> "Talking" (whether out loud or silently) and "thinking" are not concepts of the same kind; even though they are in closest connexion.

This suggests that "talking to oneself" is not somehow midway between "thinking" and "talking out loud" even though the two kinds of "talking" are still coupled. "Conversations with myself" is not comparable to "talking to myself." Would it make a difference if it were "talking *with* myself," i.e., not, for example, *admonishing* but *conversing?*

In one text Wittgenstein is prepared to use the expression "silent train of thought" (*Last Writings* v.1.

114), which is understandable because we do say such things as "I've lost my train of thought," and at this point the connection with talking is far from evident. In the following passage Wittgenstein mentions three different ways in which thinking and talking are connected, which might be reflected in different concepts.

> Remember that our language might possess a variety of different words: one for "thinking out loud"; one for thinking as one talks to oneself in the imagination; one for a pause during which something or other floats before the mind, after which, however, we are able to give a confident answer.
>
> One word for a thought expressed in a sentence; one for the lightning thought which I may later "clothe in words"; one for wordless thinking as one works. (Z 122)

The expression "lightning thought" recalls Wittgenstein's discussions of "sudden understanding" and "grasping the whole use of a word in a flash." While it is true that "Being struck is related to thinking" (*Last Writings* v.1. 717), what makes understanding coming in a flash seem queer is the picture of the whole, large use of a word being reduced to something that could be taken in in a second. This seems like what happens when one grasps a mathematical formula that may have an infinite number of applications.

> "It's as if we could grasp the whole use of a word in a flash."—And that is just what we say we do. That is to say: we sometimes describe what we do in these words. But there is nothing astonishing, nothing queer, about what happens. It becomes queer when we are led to think that the future development must in some way already be present

> in the act of grasping the use and yet isn't present.—
> For we say that there isn't any doubt that we under-
> stand the word, and on the other hand its meaning
> lies in its use. (PI 197)

The idea that the entire plan for an encyclopaedia or a
schema of universal history or a new universal field theory might occur in a single second seems extraordinary to
us because we have a picture of "containment" in which
something spread out in time could hardly be "enclosed"
in an instant in a single "brain flash." But Wittgenstein is
concerned about how the words function rather than
about the bewildering pictures that are generated.

In his *Philosophical Investigations* Wittgenstein
records what he calls *thoughts*, in the form of *remarks* or
short paragraphs. He was unable to weld these into any
natural order proceeding in a single direction, but instead
had to put them together in the form of an "album of
sketches," which would give a "picture of the landscape."
He also adds that he wanted to compare his "old
thoughts" in the *Tractatus* with these "new thoughts"
because the latter would only be seen in the right light
"against the background of my old way of thinking."
Finally, he adds that he does not want his writing to
"spare other people the trouble of thinking," but rather to
"stimulate someone to thoughts of his own."

This language in the Preface of the *Investigations*
justifies, it seems to me, raising once again the question
of the nature of Wittgenstein's own philosophic thinking
and the vast change that took place between his "old
thoughts" and his "new thoughts," his old way of thinking and his "new way," and especially what this bodes
for the future if we try to put it in a historical context.
This is the subject we turn to in the last chapter.

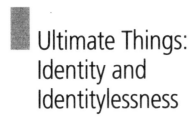

## CHAPTER 10

Ultimate Things: Identity and Identitylessness

Things do not carry their identities around inside of them.

Eric Gutkind

Where does the power of metaphysics come from? Why has it lasted so long? The answer to these questions, as we can see from studying the philosophy of Wittgenstein (though he himself did not put it this way), turns around the question of *identity*. Metaphysics begins in Plato and Aristotle with the concept of *self-identity*, which defines Being. Plato speaks of *onto, the things that really exist* (which also has the meaning of *that which one has, property, fortune*), and *onti tou ontos*, the *really real;* and also of *autos*, the *original things*, or *self-existing things*, and of *auto kath auto (in-and-by-itself)*. This is the true language of metaphysics. It is concerned with the *really real*, that which exists *in and by itself*, what has true Being, or, as the Buddhists call it, *own-Being*, or *Being from the other side*. We might suggest that it is, in a way, *doubled Being,* or the *Beingness of Being.* (It conjures up a picture of a thing "fitting into itself," or *self-existing.*)

When this is given a more systematically logical statement by Aristotle, the concept that emerges is *self-identity,* and now *that which really exists* is that which is *identical with itself.* And we have what has come down to us as Aristotle's First Law of Thought, repeated ever since, and taken to be the foundation of all logic: *A thing is identical with itself,* A = A. Some commentators add: "Without this law there would be no thought," once again confusing abstract possibility with actual practice. (A note in the margin: Hegel had no difficulty in denying this "absolute Law" and "got away with it," simply modifying slightly the meaning of *logic* and *thinking,* a process carried very much further by Wittgenstein, as we will see in the next chapter.)

It must be said that if Wittgenstein had read any classical philosophy (he first read only Schopenhauer and a little later Frege), he very likely never would have taken the first steps in dealing with these metaphysical premises and the "First Law of Thought." This is the danger of reading philosophy, as he pointed out to his students: it teaches a reverential attitude toward such matters as these metaphysical premises and logical laws. If Wittgenstein had taken the steps that he did in his own thinking *after* having studied classical philosophy, I think we would have credited him with almost superhuman powers. Even that he did it without any such study is remarkable enough, though Vienna, his home city, *was* exactly the hotbed for such new ideas, and the rarefied heights of algebraic logic were not a bad place to safely practice them.

The truth remains that Wittgenstein, practically at the beginning of his philosophic career, simply *denied* the ultimate premises of Plato's and Aristotle's thought. Without having read a word of either of them, he said that there was no more meaningless statement than the statement of self-identity or A = A (and of course this covers the case of self-existence too). And then, to top it off, he denied the modern version of this metaphysical stance, as "proven" by Descartes, by saying that there is no "thinking self," that to which Descartes had attributed self-existence or in-itselfness. But these breathtaking denials are in the *Tractatus*, dictated by logical austerity and the passion for abstract algebraic analysis.

> To say of one thing that it is identical with itself is to say nothing at all. (T 5.5303)
> There is no such thing as the subject that thinks or entertains ideas. (T 5.631)

In these two statements the nerve of metaphysics is cut even though the ghost of metaphysics remains. It remains in the notion of the absolutely simple objects that, he says, are the "substance" of the world, *substance* being the Latin word for the Greek *ousia*, meaning *beingness* or *essence*. And it also remains in the metaphysical point-subject at the limits of each human being's world. At the end of the book the objects and this metaphysical subject are said to be without sense (T 6.54), thereby insuring that the metaphysics of the book is indeed ghost-like. This is what Wittgenstein was showing all along: that *metaphysics is an unnecessary doubling*. We may wonder whether it wasn't simply his good manners and respect for great traditions that prevented him from a more outright dismissal. Whatever the reason, the desire to express this matter in the deepest and most sympathetic way led to an ever more profound examination of the roots of the problem, to the ultimate benefit of everybody.

In the light of Wittgenstein's temperament and his strong religious feelings, something else comes into view, namely that, as Wittgenstein saw it, implicitly if not explicitly, metaphysics and religion (and here the word *religion* includes both Buddhism and Christianity, as well as Islam in its Sufi aspect) are in opposition and not at all, whatever may have been the case in the medieval world, allies. We can see this clearly if we realize that a central teaching of these religions, particularly in their inceptions, is something that is the very opposite of the metaphysical idea of self-identity. It is *identitylessness.* I will not labor the point with regard to Buddhism since the Buddhist doctrines of *no-self* and the *relativity of all things* are well known even though this did not prevent Buddhist philosophers from having a difficult time dealing with metaphysics. (We speak particularly of the Madhyamika and Zen traditions, the best known in the United States.) In the Christian religion it is the *kenosis* or *kenotic* tradition that most emphasizes identitylessness. But all Christians are familiar with the dictum of St. Paul: "Not I live but Christ-Spirit lives in me." It is interesting that two of Wittgenstein's mentors in religion, Tolstoi and Dostoievsky, both in their very different ways, exemplified the kenotic spirit. Wittgenstein, we are told, also read excerpts from St. John of the Cross, who made a virtual science out of "emptying" and *identitylessness.*[1]

When Wittgenstein said that although he "was not a religious man" (i.e., did not belong to any church or religious institution) he could not help seeing all problems (i.e., everything) "from a religious point of view," his friends wondered what he meant.[2] I think they missed the point that his whole philosophic outlook was religious through and through, and nowhere so much as at the central point of identitylessness. This is not to say that

Wittgenstein was able to *practice* this. On the contrary, he constantly said that his vanity (i.e., his self-image, his self-identity, his ego-self) got in the way and that it was very hard work to try to quiet it. This happened when people appropriated and then misrepresented his ideas.

But the real point is that he *knew what had to be done*, where the problem of life lay, and that if we were to be judged by some higher source, *this* is what we would be judged about: our vanity, ego, and "selfness."

The Bird of Passage

Whatever Wittgenstein's philosophy, there remained the gap between his philosophy and his life. He might, for example, tell himself that his philosophy did not stand in the way of any genuine religion. He did not think that the philosopher should belong to any "community of ideas," whether church, synagogue, political party, ideology, national or fraternal organization. But he did hope that his philosophy would not stand in the way of anybody's religious life or development. At one point, he told his friend Drury that he had tried to say daily the Lord's Prayer, which he regarded as the most remarkable prayer ever conceived, but found that he could not continue the practice.

Many people commented on these two sides of Wittgenstein: the great sense of *openness* and *freedom* that pervaded his thinking, giving students a feeling of being liberated, and the ruthless self-criticism to which he subjected himself and his ideas. (The latter sometimes spilled over into an abruptness and impatience with others, especially if, as sometimes happened, they misunderstood him in some egregious way.) It was one thing to have a philosophy of no-self and quite another to live it.

Even his genius and his freedom (perhaps the same thing) had their limits. He sometimes asked himself whether the time he had spent trying to get his thoughts in some "natural order" for publication might not have been actually wasted. Was he worried about communication and trying to find the best way possible to minimize the ever-present looming specter of misunderstanding?

It would be difficult to imagine anything more despairing than the paragraph, toward the end of the Preface to the *Investigations*, where he speaks about making his thoughts public:

> I make them public with doubtful feelings. It is not impossible that it should fall to the lot of this work, in its poverty and in the darkness of this time, to bring light into one brain or another—but, of course, it is not likely.

Years of lack of being understood at Cambridge and in the philosophic community in general (with the exception of a few close students) must have left their mark. On the other hand, his last reported saying on his deathbed six years later on April 26, 1951, the day after his sixty-second birthday was, "Tell them I've had a wonderful life."

If after having understood both the *Tractatus* and the *Philosophical Investigations* on the question of Identity and Identitylessness, we wish to say, "There are no absolute objects or subjects and no absolute identity attached to anything at all," then these statements will not be misunderstood by anyone who has seen the point. From the other side of the metaphysical/postmetaphysical divide we can look back and see where we have come from without wondering if we are still on the wrong side of the divide. We are across the divide when it seems easy and natural to do without metaphysics. (Nietzsche's fearsome dream of an abyss of nihilism between metaphysics and post-metaphysics does not have to happen at all, unless we take it that this is what has been happening during the past century. Nietzsche's romanticism, however, prevented him from seeing daily life as the · *sufficient* answer.) It cannot be said that Wittgenstein's philosophy makes us at home in a world without metaphysics (since no such world exists, and there is no substitute for having a world!). One of the most telling objections to the average modern "self" is that it is "worldless." Locked away in a false subjectivity and privacy, it is not really in relation to anything at all, neither other people nor a "world."

Wittgenstein's notorious impatience with philosophy and other philosophers (he was always advising students not to go into philosophy) quite obviously arose from the fact that philosophers were not in his eyes *open*. *His* openness to the new, to the unheard-of, made him feel that the others were in shackles. And this was especially true of the two great Panjandrums at Cambridge: Bertrand Russell and G. E. Moore. They not only could not follow the new Wittgenstein during his second sojourn at Cambridge; they could not even *begin* to understand him. (Oddly both of them regarded themselves as liberated and free spirits.) From this type of philosophy and philosopher little could be expected. It was no joke when Wittgenstein told Norman Malcolm that he preferred the silliness of Hollywood movies, Street and Smith detective novels, and P. G. Wodehouse to the cleverness of the dons at the Trinity College high table, trying to put each other down.

What justifies applying the words "openness," "inner freedom" and "identitylessness in thinking" to

Wittgenstein was his non-attachment, his *Gelassenheit*, to borrow a word from Heidegger, who took it from Meister Eckhart. Being in his company, people felt this spontaneity. Not only was he a *rara avis*, a rare bird, but something more vulnerable and more precious, a *Wandervogel* (the word was his), a wander-bird, a bird of passage, fair game to be shot at by anybody, and not to be imprisoned by any dogma or doctrine. In practical life, human, all too human—proud, irritable, inconsiderate, "difficult"—but in philosophy, independent, marvelously fresh and new, and, above all, courageous to a degree quite beyond our comprehension. We hide our amazement behind the word so often applied to him: *genius.* But what do we mean by this word? Undoubtedly that, like Socrates, he listened to a voice that was not only the voice of conscience (though perhaps that too), but also an intellectual source that he would not have been immodest enough to call spirit. The genius is the person who can live *without an identity*, at least in music, poetry, philosophy, etc.

The philosopher Karl Britton, already referred to, described Wittgenstein's Saturday morning classes, first at G. E. Moore's home, and then at his own rooms in Whewell Court, Cambridge. Britton mentions Wittgenstein's impatience and then adds:

> The most characteristic of all his attitudes was a very quiet, very intense stare—suddenly adopted and leading to a slow deliberate utterance of some new point. Very often he got thoroughly "stuck," appealed in vain to his hearers to help him out; he would walk about in despair murmuring "I'm a fool. I'm a fool." And such was the difficulty of the topics he discussed that all this struggle did not seem to us

> to be in the least excessive. (Britton, *Listener*, June
> 16, 1955)

When he gets "stuck" the inspiration is failing, the
shaman's tongue falls silent, and he is helpless. But then
again comes the "very quiet, very intense stare" which
we would like to contrast with the "vacant stare" the
philosopher assumes when he is trying to focus his attention on, for example, his own consciousness (PI 412).

Britton confesses that he, like others, would occa-
sionally doze off for a minute or two now and then, for it
is all too evident that hardly anyone (and maybe no one)
understood what was going on at all, though they certainly knew that *something* of importance was going on,
the very reaction students still have on looking into these
books for the first time. What impressed Britton, as it still
does the students, was that

> often one came away feeling that a tremendous
> effort had been made and little if anything achieved,
> but of course looking back on the series, one can
> see how much had been achieved. (Ibid.)

It was a mind focused like a laser beam that impressed
them. Some said they had never *seen* a man thinking
before. And when a breathtakingly simple and transpar-
ently clear pronouncement would suddenly come forth,
even if it happened only rarely, everyone in the room
would experience an excitement and quickening, and an
intoxicating sense of suddenly being released into a
greater freedom.

Small wonder that this all looked like a cult to more
orthodox Cambridgeites. Something was going on, and
one could be either impressed or scornful. What people
outside could *not* see so easily was the discipline of this

mind, the combination of profundity and common sense, literalism and imagination, outrageously new ideas clothed in the most innocent-sounding short sentences. As it has seemed to Wittgenstein's readers since, it was worthwhile to hack one's way through the jungle for weeks, suddenly to emerge (even if only for a brief time) into a place of miraculous light. So must other young men and women have felt listening to Kant or Hegel or Socrates or Saint Augustine or Christ or Buddha or Mohammed. For these people were all in their very different ways *mouthpieces of identitylessness*, seized by something to be said that had no truck with their egos. The "chaos" that Wittgenstein said it was necessary to be at home in (CV 65e) and to go down into each morning (CV 2e), what else was this but the "abyss of freedom" to which the supreme teachers have given such various names? This was the cauldron of the originality of his philosophy, and at the same time the source of the *courage* that he said was the one indispensable quality, the way in which we *pay for* thoughts (CV 52e).

Early in his philosophic life Wittgenstein coined a metaphor that continued to haunt his philosophy. He said that his aim was to "show the fly the way out of the fly-bottle," obviously referring to the human self, and in its late manifestation the Cartesian "thinking self" or, still more recently, the "existentialist self." Abandoning the "thinking self," and the identity and self-identity that supported it, took him half-way there. But in this matter, half-way is no better than no way at all. *Dropping the private self entirely, together with the inner world and mental objects and processes, was the required whole liberation.*

What does *identitylessness* mean? Mainly non-attachment, as this was understood by philosophers from Meister Eckhart to Heidegger. And this means non-identification, not to be identified with *family, tribe, nation, class, people, profession, gender* and, of course, above all, with *possessions,* including *knowledge, ego,* and *self.* This is the principle that unites religion (in which it is called *humility*) and philosophy (in which it is called *scepticism*), Buddhism and Christianity (which both require giving up ego and self), Sufism and Taoism, Tolstoi and Dostoievsky. Attachment is severed at the root when the ego disappears. And ego is in not a small part vanity.

What happens in philosophy is, of course, not the same thing as what happens in life, though they are closely related. This is the significance of Wittgenstein's lifelong struggle with his *vanity,* which is enshrined in the Preface to PI where he confesses that it "stung my vanity" to have his thoughts (his results) circulated by others, "variously misunderstood, more or less mangled or watered down" (PI ixe), as if thoughts or philosophic results could be a "possession"! He recognized the absurdity of the Leibniz-Newton battle, lasting for years, over the question of who first discovered the calculus. And he flatly stated how he felt about what is now called "intellectual property," something that presumably some Marxists have not discovered yet, in either the economic or the religious sense.

> If my remarks do not bear a stamp which marks them as mine,—I do not wish to lay any further claim to them as my property. (PI xe)

With Wittgenstein the remark that "Ambition is the death of thought" (CV 77e) is not an empty bromide, but a spiritual discovery that ego stands in the way of the inner abandonment and freedom, which is necessary not only for poetry, art, and religion, but also for thinking and philosophy.

What Is a Human Being?

Closely connected with the question of identity, though of a different kind, is another metaphysical question which, because of its "scientific" or pseudo-scientific form, has become the principal philosophic question of our time, the so-called mind-body problem. This involves the clash of two pictures, which seem equally vivid and real but cannot be fitted together: one is the picture of the human brain with its billions of neural cells and nerve connections, appearing as a greyish mass the size of a soccer ball; the other is a picture of an equally vast assemblage of images, memories, sensations, ideas, thoughts and feelings, which we believe are somehow related to this physical organ. When we are able to map the brain and locate areas and centers particularly related to these various mental activities, the situation is no better since the complete discordance between what still appear to be two entirely different kinds of "realities" remains. What could possibly connect an experienced sensation of red, for example, with a chemical or electrical discharge down a neural pathway? This is the so-called problem—between mentalist and physicalist facts. Or are there two sets of "facts" here, or are we being misled by *that* word?

This entire "problem" will have to appear in a new light before we can even begin to imagine what is wrong with it, how our words and our pictures have seduced us into a phantomlike difficulty. A transformation of both the images and the "relation" between them will have to take place to disentangle the difficulty. It is no accident that the metaphysical and epistemological crisis should come to a head right here, in the question of the *image of the human being.* How will this transformation come about?

First, Wittgenstein prefers the word *soul (Seele)* to the word *mind (Gemüt* or *Geist)*. It is easier to unite *body* and *soul* than *body* and *mind* since we tend to think of *mind* as "in the head" and *soul* as "spread throughout the body." Locating the *soul*, people are likely to point to the heart or the chest, the traditional seat of thought, for example, in the Hebrew language. In one text Wittgenstein mentions Luther saying that "faith" was located "just below the left nipple." Other religions, such as Hinduism, locate it slightly to the right of the heart.

The significance of this change to *body* and *soul* may be somewhat obscured by the decision of Wittgenstein's official English translator, Elizabeth Anscombe, to translate, wrongly, I am told by German speakers, *Seele (soul)* as *mind* in more than fifteen cases. (In the bilingual edition where the German is on the facing pages, this can be corrected by consulting the German, but not in the all-English editions.) In any case, we should not miss the point that a first small step in dealing with the body-mind problem is to see a human being again, as the ancient and medieval worlds did, in terms of body-soul rather than body-mind.

We must, of course, deal with the question of whether thinking, imagining, perceiving, etc., takes place "in the head" or "in the whole body." We do not say, "My brain sees" or "My brain thinks," but "I see" and "I think". *I* is a word that stands not for *soul*, but for *ego* or *self*. It may be helpful to distinguish between ego and self, the former being the self-image at the center of the latter. Some introduce the term "*person*" to stand for the whole of the human being, though this may lead to confusion with *personality* and also make it difficult to draw the important distinction between *personal* and *impersonal*.

How are we to conceive of the body-soul unity? This

dictum gives us the best clue:

> The human body is the best picture of the human
> soul. (PI 178)

The body is the visible expression or manifestation
(Wittgenstein says in one place *gesture*) of the soul. This
is a key formulation ramifying in many directions. It even
requires that we learn to look differently, to look at the
human body in a different way. (Note that Wittgenstein
says *body*, not *face* or *eyes*. The face is an epitomization
of the body, as the eyes are of the face, but it is the
whole body that is the primary manifestation.)

In this physiognomic conception of the human
being as the one body-soul, it looks as if we actually *see*
the soul in the expressiveness of the body. It almost
seems as if Wittgenstein has reversed the ancient
Aristotelean view that the soul is the form of the body,
turning it into the Goethean formula that the body is the
visible expression of the soul. When we look at people
in a deep enough way we actually *see* them as *ensouled*.
Their postures, their walks, their expressions and gestures, their voices, clothes, etc. Sometimes in an unexpected moment, when we look deeply, or as someone
passes in front of us, we may get a total sense of that
person from all these bodily clues.

We may be approaching again another meaning of
the expression *form of life*. Consider another cryptic
Wittgenstein statement, much discussed:

> If a lion could talk we could not understand him. (PI
> 223)

In other words, if we were able to record all lion communication and conversation, visual as well as audible,
and were able to translate this into English, we would

still not be able to understand it. Why not? Because a lion is a different form of life from us and too different for us to be able to find our footing with it.

On the other hand, and this is Wittgenstein talking and not a nineteenth-century exponent of the pathetic fallacy, we *do* have enough in common with a lion to be able to recognize in it to some extent a kindred soul. We see in that body and that demeanour something noble, kingly, and prideful. This is a shared part of spirit. But is there also what we cannot comprehend? A degree of *felineness* past the limits of our intelligence? It is not that we cannot *feel* what it would be like to be a lion, a bat or a snake, as some philosophers have suggested, but that the spirit or soul of the lion in its manifestation does not come within our ken. Something similar happens with other human beings who are mentally ill, or of a too strangely different religion or culture.

Suppose that the lion nature were such that it could talk, but also that when anyone mentioned the weather it would immediately attack that person. If it were required that lions have culture in order to have such a custom, then that would be part of the supposition. Yet something else might be required too. Would a lion have a different body if it were to talk? But then surely it would cease being a lion. A creature with a lion body that talks is easy enough to imagine, at least with the help of Disney. But such a creature that talks lion-talk is impossible for us to imagine. In Wittgenstein's early *Notebooks* we find this:

> Now is it true (following the psycho-physical conception) that my character is expressed only in the build of *my* body or brain and not equally in the build of the whole of the rest of the world?

This contains a salient point.

This parallelism, then, really exists between my spirit, i.e. spirit, and the world.

Only remember that the spirit of the snake, of the lion, is *your* spirit. For it is only from yourself that you are acquainted with spirit at all.

Now of course the question is why I have given a snake just this spirit.

And the answer to this can only lie in the psycho-physical parallelism: If I were to look like the snake and to do what it does, then I should be such-and-such.

The same with the elephant, with the fly, with the wasp.

But the question arises whether even here, my body is not on the same level with that of the wasp. . . .

Is this the solution of the puzzle why men have always believed that there was one spirit common to the whole world?

And in that case it would, of course, also be common to lifeless things too. (N/85e)

This was written during the First World War, in 1916. By the time thirty years later we get to the "talking lion" (PI 223), instead of an overall pan-cosmic theory about two realities running along in parallel (a traditional metaphysical post-Cartesian picture), which invites endless arguments because it is not convincing, we have a multiplicity of *forms of life* in which what we *see* are creatures that are as much ensouled bodies as embodied souls because that is exactly what we see when we look at them. We are no longer putting forward a theory about how a mentalistic picture can be reconciled with a physicalist one, in which both pictures appear complete in themselves and there is so conspicuously no connection. Descartes regarded God as the *connector*, as if introduced for that purpose. His followers Malebranche and Guelinx saw an inexplicable, miraculous preestablished harmony between two realities that never affected each other at all. But there is an ancient saying that the exit is where the entrance was, and we need to disavow the Pythagorean-Platonic starting point that separated the two to begin with. Body and soul or body and mind as two ultimate separate substances cannot be united. We cannot unite spatio-temporal "matter" and non-material "mind"—these two metaphysical absolutes. But Wittgenstein's philosophy shows that we *can* unite the *physiognomically expressive body as seen and the language-meaning mind as spoken.* In other words the human body that we see and of which we speak is just such a whole expressed in two ways.

PART THREE
Old and New Thoughts

## CHAPTER 11

Two Ways of Thinking

Wittgenstein said that he often felt as if he was writing for people who had not yet been born, who would breathe a different air and think in a different way.

G. H. von Wright

To understand the change from the "old" to the "new way of thinking" in Wittgenstein (terms he uses in the Preface to PI) we must get a clear view of each of these ways. This means we must look at the character of the dominant strain in Western thought which Wittgenstein came to reject and contrast this with the new method that he adopted. The old method we will call the "method of abstraction," the method by which the *Tractatus* was arrived at. It has been the dominant "progressive" force in modern mathematics and logic, intimately connected with modern science, as distinct from Greek science or from what may come in the future. The new way of thinking we will call, for reasons to be discussed later, that of *metaphoric connection*.

Abstraction and
Metaphoric Connection

The "method of abstraction" refers to the gradual
spread into one field of mathematics after another and
then into logic of algebraic methods and the algebraic
way of thinking, which substitutes contentless or meaningless formal signs, defined by their places in formal
systems, for natural numbers, geometrical curves and
shapes, trigonometric functions, functions of the calculus,
and finally the propositional functions of logic. By this
process mathematics, logic and scientific theory were cut
off, as they were not in Greek science, from direct com-
prehensibility and, in a wider sense, the *natural*, the *cultural* and the *traditional.*

Wittgenstein's *Tractatus* may be seen as the final
breaking point in this history, the place where the analytic algebraic development reached its zenith in attenuation, nearly empty formalization and, finally,
self-contradiction. It is the place and moment where the
old way of thinking was (in Wittgenstein's own image)
condensed into purest crystal, a lifeless perfection soon
to be shattered.

Before we examine more closely this breaking-point
(the "crystal" shattered), we must put the *Tractatus* in its
own context as the successor of Whitehead's *Treatise on
Universal Algebra* (Cambridge, 1898) and Whitehead and
Russell's monumental three-volume formulation of an
algebra of propositional logic as the foundation of arithmetic, the *Principia Mathematica* (Cambridge,
1910–1913) (which, however, was a self-admitted failure
because it required two non-logical axioms and for other
reasons which Wittgenstein and others were later to
raise).[1]

These books themselves are in the direct line of descent from the beginnings of algebra in the arithmetic of the third-century Greek Alexandrian mathematician Diophantus, who introduced just one, and no more, unknown term in his equations which was itself an *abbreviation* of a word.[2] Leaving aside the intermediary roles of Hindu and Arab mathematics, the decisive step toward modern algebra was taken by the Renaissance mathematician Franciscus Vieta (1540–1603), who made a purely symbolic algebra in which meaningless letters played the largest role. The historian of mathematics E. T. Bell described it as a kind of mathematics in which meanings of terms could be totally disregarded until a stage was reached in which we wanted to interpret them. Of Vieta's accomplishment, he said:

> The experience gained through centuries of laborious trial is condensed in mechanical processes which can be applied and manipulated with a minimum of thinking. (*Development of Mathematics* [New York: 1945], 124)

(And of course we now know where this will lead.)

Descartes' Algebraic Geometry in which equations with unknowns (variables) replace geometrical figures is intimately associated with theoretical modern physics, along with the "ideal ratios" of differential and integral calculus, descended from the Greek mathematician Eudoxus's "method of exhaustion," but again expressed in universal abstract symbols.

The nineteenth century saw the "algebra-izing" of logic, beginning with George Boole's logic of classes in which the elements of the classes (i.e., the meanings of the classes) were treated as irrelevant and only "unions" and "intersections" were considered. In Charles Peirce's logic of relations and Whitehead's, Frege's, and Russell's logic of propositions, the same process of substituting empty symbols for the concrete meanings of the relations and propositions was carried out. It was dawning on everybody that both mathematics and logic had no content at all, or the content could be disregarded as irrelevant. Irrelevant to what? To the power gained by forcible abstraction. Modern science starts with this hybris.

There is another aspect of the development of modern mathematics which has greatly strengthened the thrust toward ideal abstraction. This is the focus on axiomatization, putting all branches of mathematics into axiomatic form. *Principia Mathematica* not only attempted to unify arithmetic (seen as the basis of all mathematics) and logic by putting them both into algebraic symbols, it also wanted to axiomatize both subjects into one vast empty system. Here we go back to just one source, Euclid's geometry, which arranged all Greek geometry into a single deductive system based on twenty-three Definitions, five Postulates and five Axioms or "Common Notions." (The distinction between "postulates" and "axioms" is no longer accepted.) An axiom is a statement accepted without proof from which all the other statements of a system can be derived, in the way that Euclid had done and Aristotle had systematized in his formal deductive logic.

The program put forward by David Hilbert (1862–1943) to axiomatize all branches of mathematics, as Peano (1858–1932) had axiomatized arithmetic and Russell and Whitehead logic (though for Hilbert logic was not the basis for arithmetic) shows how axiomatizing cut across other disagreements. Deductions can be made in systems that have no content or meaning, provided that the symbols are used consistently and the axioms are consistent with each other. The deductive relations are also empty of content.

What happens here is that *necessity too becomes empty of content*, a purely formal relation, like the deduction that whatever applies to all elements in a set applies to any element in it. Necessity is divorced from human life and is either identified with deterministic laws of physics (Hobbes, Spinoza) or becomes a purely logical relation (Hume, Wittgenstein). In the human world where necessity is connected with death, taxes and brute force, what is a person to make of this from the *Tractatus*:

> There is no compulsion making one thing happen because another has happened. The only necessity that exists is *logical* necessity. (T 6.37)

(Have the philosophers gone mad? Total logical necessity with total factual arbitrariness is a combination that doesn't relate to anything human.)

Empty signs, combined only in deductive necessity as a scientific model, was a gruel too rarefied for Whitehead the philosopher, however much it described the situation in mathematics. In his Preface to the *Universal Algebra* he wrote:

> Mathematics in its widest signification is the development of all types of formal, necessary, deductive reasoning. The reasoning is formal in the sense that the meaning of propositions forms no part of the investigation. The sole concern of mathematics is the inference of proposition from proposition. The business of mathematics is simply to follow the rules (of inference). In this sense all mathematical reasoning is necessary, namely it has followed the rule. (vi)

How far can these claims go in implicating a whole culture? Whitehead draws the line here as Wittgenstein
could not or would not.

> The ideal of mathematics should be to erect a calcu-
> lus to facilitate reasoning in connection with every
> province of thought, or of external experience, in
> which the succession of thoughts, or of events can
> be definitely ascertained and precisely stated. So that
> all serious thought, which is not philosophy or
> inductive reasoning, or imaginative literature, shall
> be mathematics developed by means of a calculus.
> (vi, vii)

Here Whitehead excludes philosophy from the dominant
cultural reality of the age and is willing to put it in a sub-
ordinate position, a step that Wittgenstein was not willing
to take. Instead Wittgenstein's philosophy attempted to
bring out into the open that very spirit of scientism, its
mathematical essence, to which Whitehead had made
such a major contribution. Wittgenstein wanted to show,
for better and worse, its limitations. The passion for logical purity, which meant knowledge completely grasped
and possessed by being totally simplified, universalized
and axiomatized, was his passion too. But he was equally certain that this had nothing at all to do with ethics
(nor with the "truth of solipsism"—i.e., of direct individual experience), and this too should be made clear.

In the *Tractatus* Wittgenstein not only embraced the
spirit of abstraction, but also carried it further in unheard-
of ways, making of it a crystalline structure of impenetra-
ble hardness and inhuman lustre. Six things in particular
stand out as such further contributions to abstract logical
purity:

(1) He introduces "truth tables," a mechanical way of laying out the "truth possibilities" of elementary propositions. For example, between two such propositions there are sixteen possible logical relations or operations, defining sixteen possible "truth functions" for the ensuing complex propositions, etc. (T 5.101).

(2) He reduces the sixteen logical relations or operations to one basic one, which he calls General Negation or the "general form of a truth function." This is negation that does not treat "negation of negation" as affirmation, but simply reiterated negation (T 5.502).

(3) He recognizes that in the world consisting only of facts, the logical forms of these facts cannot themselves be further facts and so cannot be represented, as facts are, by being structurally mirrored; instead they must be *shown* (i.e., must remain implicit in the structures, instead of being able to be spoken about). In this way he avoided the hierarchy of languages, which Russell believed necessary in order for language to speak about language and another language about that one, and so on *ad infinitum.*

(4) He recognized two kinds of truth only: the isomorphic one-to-one mapping of symbol-structures onto object-structures that produced the simple (elementary) propositions, and the complex propositions produced by the logical relatings of the simple ones.

(5) He puts all necessity in the realm of logical possibilities (and there are no other kinds of possibilities and these *are the same for world, thought, and language*), while the realm of facts consists of whichever of these possibilities *happen* to have come into existence by sheer contingency. All necessity

belongs to the hidden logical possibilities and all chance or contingency to the actual facts. Necessity completely formal, facts completely absurd!

(6) The only kind of individual direct immediate experience that remains in such a world is that of solipsism, which, of course, cannot be spoken about. The individual human being (as other than factual) is reduced to the absolutely single private point of the *I*. This is the "self" that goes with the purely abstract logical world of modern science—the "self" in terms of which we all (without knowing why) suffer. Alienation and isolation of "selves" cannot go further.

In outlining the above six points it will be noted that we have not mentioned the word *meaning* though this is what the *Tractatus* is really all about: filling in the meanings that had been left out, but are nevertheless implied (or we might better say, presupposed) by the pure abstractions of science and algebraized logic. Just what has been left out of logic and mathematics in their triumphant progress toward pure abstraction (namely, meanings) is just what Wittgenstein wants to bring in *at the end*, when the meanings themselves will be the most abstract. We have known from the time of Euclid what the most abstract meanings are; they are geometrical *points*, algebraized in modern geometry, logically universalized by Russell. These are the logical points or *objects* of the *Tractatus* to be named by utterly simple names. Simple propositions will then be combinations of these names mapped onto absolutely similar combinations of the points or objects. Nothing, it seems, could be simpler than this: (1) names have meanings only by referring to (or designating) *objects* (logical points in logical space, which is generalized property spaces); (2) names have these meanings only in combinations of these meanings, which are propositions; (3) propositions have *sense* (a second kind of meaning) in the way that an arrow does; they say that things are a certain way, which then may be true or false (the things or objects may be that way or may not be that way). Wittgenstein was unable to produce a *single example of an object!* The present writer prefers to think of them as what corresponds to the coordinates for identifying properties in different kinds of property spaces. The upshot, in any case, is that even the meanings of the logical abstractions in the *Tractatus* have no "content." *All* the "content" is in the "solipsistic" experience.[3]

The Crystal Shattered

If we have to marvel at how a logically perfect language (purely formal, purely deductive) became the essence of the world, we have to marvel even more at how Wittgenstein, having been gripped by such a picture with its long historical momentum, was ever able to break its hold on him. We are fortunate, however, because we have his own description of the change from the method of abstract analysis to that of "rearranging to make surveyable." Three passages contrasting the two methods will be helpful. In the first he is talking about what essence has come to mean to him in the new way, by contrast with the old way: Essence has come to mean

> something that already lies open to view and that becomes surveyable by a rearrangement, (not) something that lies beneath the surface. (Not) something that lies within, which we see when we look *into* the thing, and which an analysis digs out. (PI 92)

The imagery of *rearranging* instead of *digging* is vivid
and to the point. The search for the "behind-the-world
reality," which Nietzsche so brilliantly exposed at the end
of his life as the central idea in the history of Western
metaphysics, here takes the form of a "below-the-world"
foundation. It is much more plausible to believe that
everything we need is already in plain view. As Nietzsche
thought too, we have been chasing phantasms, chimeras,
and illusions in trying to find the super-real, and it is time
now to open our eyes and look around.

A second quotation gives a simple and natural reason for preferring the new method, but one that is easily
overlooked:

> We see that what we call "sentence" and "lan-
> guage" has not the formal unity that I imagined, but
> is the family of structures more or less related to one
> another.—But what becomes of logic now? Its rigour
> seems to be giving way here.—But in that case
> doesn't logic altogether disappear?—For how can it
> lose its rigour? Of course not by our bargaining any
> of its rigour out of it.—The *preconceived idea* of
> crystalline purity can only be removed by turning
> our whole examination round. (One might say: the
> axis of reference of our examination must be rotat-
> ed, but about the fixed point of our real need.)
>
> The philosophy of logic speaks of sentences
> and words in exactly the sense in which we speak
> of them in ordinary life when we say e.g. "Here is a
> Chinese sentence", or "No, that only looks like writ-
> ing; it is actually just an ornament" and so on.
>
> We are talking about the spatial and temporal
> phenomenon of language, not about some non-spa-
> tial, non-temporal phantasm.

> [Note in margin: Only it is possible to be interested
> in a phenomenon in a variety of ways]. (PI 108)

The *imperialism* of logic, demanding everything or nothing, is mentioned here, but the most interesting words in
this passage are perhaps "our real need." We don't really
need the metaphysical phantasms. What we *really* need,
that is, what will really satisfy us, is the "complete clarity"
which we will get when we are able to take in (as it
were in one view) the wholly natural and normal ways in
which words genuinely relate.

The third quotation fixes this point by giving itself a
far more satisfying description of the word *description*
than the tortured Russell-inspired "isomorphic mapping."
Since many maps are possible of any town or terrain, the
idea of a perfect map, as, for example, a topological set,
is so far away from any ordinary description that the discussion winds up with this word itself, in this bizarre
usage, seeming irrelevant.

> It was true to say that our considerations could
> not be scientific ones. . . . And we may not advance
> any kind of theory. There must not be anything
> hypothetical in our considerations. We must do
> away with all *explanation*, and description alone
> must take its place. And this description gets its
> light, that is to say its purpose, from the philosophi-
> cal problems. (PI 109)

What will satisfy our real need is a philosophical problem
vanishing into the everydayness of normal human intelligence so that we are not left with a substitute confusion.
Rearranging what we already know means saying, "This
(concept, image, word usage) belongs with that one and
not, as you have been led to think, with that other one."

For example, "Don't think of *pain* on the model of an inner object, but think of it on the model of a word used as further learned pain behavior." Or, "Don't think of *certainty* as a high degree of knowledge or belief; think of it as daily trustings or takings-for-granted." Or, "Don't think of *rituals* as attempts to control nature (unsuccessfully); think of them as gesture-language or expressions of bodily reactions to important occasions or phenomena." In each of these examples there has been a rearrangement which people familiar with the English language will be able to understand. If the description of the ordinary way of speaking has been done carefully enough, we should be relieved of the temptations to pursue unreal problems down unreal roads.

In contrasting the two methods, the *analytic* one and the *rearrangement* one, Wittgenstein's old and new ways of thinking, I cannot think of sharper and more vivid contrast than that supplied by his altogether serious remark that "A six-year-old boy knows as much about the foundations of arithmetic as Bertrand Russell does." Here we have the three volumes of a twentieth-century mathematical logic masterpiece simply put to one side as being on the wrong track completely. It is no wonder that Russell, for his part, felt that Wittgenstein had given up serious philosophy completely. The word *philosophy* must have simply changed its meaning too drastically to be even the same subject. (Similar things were said about twentieth century nonrepresentational art and atonal music—that they are not *art* or *music* at all. And some physicists have reacted the same way to some of the newer theories in the quantum domain.)

If we look through the *Principia Mathematica* we will find the simple arithmetic equation $1 + 1 = 2$ expressed in the symbols x, y, and z and the symbols for the various logical connectives and punctuation. Whitehead and Russell are certainly under the impression that, because their algebraic version is more general or universal, it is therefore more "fundamental" and should be thought of as providing a "logical foundation" for arithmetic.

What is Wittgenstein's new view? That the so-called "foundation" is an illusion. Arithmetic needs no such "foundation," and such "foundation" leaves it without what it really needs (or we really need): the actual application of these signs built into the very learning and meaning of the signs (which is what the six-year-old boy, if he has learned his addition, has indeed learned).

The "purity" misleads us because we do not realize that what has been lost in direct piecemeal applicability (this natural kind of meaning) is not made up for by the greater formal universality. For, having once lost the connection between theory and practice it may not be possible to get it back again (just as if the human head, or part of it, started to function independently of the rest of the body). The requirement that meaning can only come from a whole system that had been cut off from the start turns out to be only *imposing* an abstract picture further and further from the reality.

As everyone who has studied contemporary philosophy and ideology knows, there is everywhere the fatal split between *theory* and *practice*. Marxists, for example, have long been aware that this was the Achilles heel of their philosophy, which showed itself most horrendously in what happened to Communism in Russia and Eastern Europe. Much vague talk about the need for a "humanistic" and "ethical" Communism transpired without anyone challenging the prestige conferred upon "pure" theory by contemporary mathematics and science.

It was a subject that greatly concerned Marxist revisionist thinkers, among them especially Wittgenstein's friend and fellow Cambridge professor Piero Sraffa, to whom Wittgenstein said he was indebted for the "most consequential ideas" of the *Philosophical Investigations* (PI xe). From Sraffa's writings on economics we can see that it was the question of bringing back together theory and practice by taking as his starting point the "reproducibility of commodities" rather than human needs, which focused his thought.

In abandoning the "theory of value" with its idealized abstract picture of the "needing subject" on one side and "scarce commodities" on the other, Sraffa was giving up in economics the very subject-object framework Wittgenstein was giving up in philosophy. In his very short (ninety pages) arcane book *Production of Commodities by Means of Commodities* (1960), Sraffa set up as a starting point for economics something like Wittgenstein's autonomous grammar, *production that recycles itself.* We can imagine that Wittgenstein and Sraffa in their conversations were both fighting their ways out of theoretical impasses created by two starting points that separated theory and practice.

It should be noted that the theory-practice dilemma, in, however, a reverse fashion from the way it appears in Marxism, plagues American philosophy and particularly American pragmatism. When it does not deteriorate into sheer opportunism (perhaps saved by a residual Puritan ethic), pragmatism puts so much emphasis on practice that it leaves hardly any room for theory at all. The whole world knows that this is its strength and weakness, that it has no way of looking ahead, no comprehensive theories. And it is also common knowledge that American thinkers, with the striking exceptions of

Charles Sanders Peirce and Josiah Willard Gibbs, have been notoriously weak on theory, but geniuses as inventors and engineers. The only questions they "hear" are *Does it work?* and *How does it work?* No criterion counts more than success and no knowledge and understanding more than know-how. Communism could not get from ideology (which was already supposed to be a combination of theory and practice) to practice; pragmatism cannot get from practice to theory.

What we can learn from Wittgenstein about this is how profoundly we have to understand something "on the surface" to find the place where theory and practice are indeed united as they were originally in the six-year-old's arithmetic classroom, before the purely theoretical mathematicians intervened. For him Russell and Whitehead's great book, which he had at first followed unquestioningly, became an object lesson in the wrong way of thinking because it was willing to get further and further away even from possible practice for the sake of a "machine-like" (i.e., meaningless and thoughtless) arithmetic and logic. The robot calculator, the faceless bureaucrat, and the brutal Gauletier are all functional brothers under the skin.

When in the face of the marvellous intellectual achievement of the *Principia* (though it was, as it turned out, an achievement in the direction of mechanization and computerization) Wittgenstein had the courage (or impudence) to say that "a six-year-old boy knows as much about the foundations of arithmetic as Bertrand Russell does," he was indeed expressing the truth of the matter, for there is no *real unity* between arithmetic and logic in the *Principia*, but only a theoretical unity between two ghostlike wraiths of themselves. Lacking the immediate self-applying applicability at every point, everything hangs in the air. On the other hand, if our real need, what we really want, were mechanization and power, then we would be moving in the right direction toward further separating mind and body, theory and practice, abstract thought and meaningful thought. This was not, of course, what Russell and Whitehead had in mind. To denigrate pure theory would have seemed to them virtually sacrilege. But, of course pure theory is not being denigrated, only the pretense that it is the *foundation* of anything so important as arithmetic.

The question of where and how theory and practice are united receives its answer in several ways in Wittgenstein's philosophy, perhaps most dramatically symbolized in the six-year-old's learning of arithmetic, for he learns it, we may presume, with apples and oranges, crayons and pencils, as demonstrations and applications of what the numbers and equations mean and can refer to. To begin arithmetic by talking about set theory, as is done in some schools today, is the wrong approach. It is as if we were to begin teaching a child language by teaching it Esperanto rather than its own mother tongue. (So strong is the hidden rage of abstraction against nature!) What seems so up-to-date is simply on the wrong track, for it says to the child: "The foundation lies in abstraction (or perhaps even a calculating machine) rather than in culture and convention." This artificiality and violation of organic needs and feelings may perhaps stay with the child for the rest of its life. Worse than this, it says: "Your roots are in mechanical electronics, which perhaps you will never really understand though there are those who do, and the priesthood of science has given it to you."

Wittgenstein, with the help of the revisionist Marxist Piero Sraffa, reunited theory and practice where it most needs to be done, in the learning of language and arithmetic. He found the answer to the "rage of abstraction" in the place where the language-game of arithmetic is first taught and where it may be experienced as an intelligible link between language and the world, and not merely as a computer operation.

The *Tractatus* itself is an object lesson, not only in the falling apart of the *public* and *private*, each into its own absolute punctiform, the logical point objects and the solipsist point *I*, but also in the falling apart of the *theoretical* and the *practical* (though Wittgenstein avoids the words *theory* and *theoretical*, applied to his own philosophy, like the plague). The "practical" was ordinary everyday language that somehow had to be shown to be derivable by the logical operations from the ideal logical language. He did not actually even begin to show how this could be done in practice. If the ideal language was simple and universal enough, then the complete logical derivations *must* be possible even though nobody had performed them.

If, for example, we take an ordinary sentence, *John loves Mary*, and for the moment ignore the difficulties of identifying *John* and *Mary* in terms of their *worlds* and so treat them as point-objects, and we allow ourselves to think of *love* as a symbolic heart placed between the two names, then we still have the almost insuperable task of translating this "heart" into logical relations, especially if we refuse to settle for a behavioristic definition of "love" such as, for example, "regularity of sexual relations." If we write *John loves Mary* as J-RL-M, we are nowhere near what we want, which is a particular x and a particular y, related by a particular R. To my knowledge nobody has done this for a single ordinary sentence, and perhaps it cannot be done. The logical reduction to simple qualities, which may be structurally represented, is of almost insuperable difficulty, although this has never lessened the impressiveness of Wittgenstein's book.

We have been speaking about what Wittgenstein himself calls his "new way of thinking" in contrast with his old way, and this is very much part of his break with the "spirit of the age." The old way we have described as adhering to the methods of abstraction or generality through abstraction, a method predominating in the *algebraization* of mathematics since the Renaissance, a method that has extended not only to geometry, including projective geometry and trigonometry, but also to functions, arithmetic, mechanics, and finally in the last century to all the newly created branches of logic itself, including the logics of classes, relations and propositions. We said that Wittgenstein's *Tractatus* can be seen as the last final attenuation, when it attempted to bring back in the one thing missing from all the algebraization—meaning.

We saw the *Tractatus* as having achieved something so refined, so pure, that it had virtually lost touch with practice altogether. It was as if Wittgenstein was saying, "You want abstraction? I'll give you abstraction. We will see what kind of a world goes with, or is implied by, or is presupposed by this universal algebra." But, as we have seen, the air was too thin on the empyrean heights where Russell, Frege and Wittgenstein at that time dwelled like acolytes of the religion of logical exactitude. As Wittgenstein discovered, the logical reductionist method would not even work for color predicate statements. (It was impossible to find a simple coordinate space for colors, the next most simple thing to space and time—presumably.)

What was this new method, which Wittgenstein called the "rearrangement of what we already know," that is, conceptual or grammatical clarification? We need to consider what are the essential differences between attaining generality and synoptic understanding through the method of abstract reduction, and obtaining it through the method of conceptual clarification. Does the latter expression in a sense deceive us by covering up something more important? What is the core of the real alternative to abstract reduction?

An expression that comes to mind is *metaphoric connection*, a method of unification and generality that is certainly non-reductive and preserves meanings. In fact *it unites in terms of meanings*. A powerful metaphor, one that can grip a whole lifetime or a whole age, may be as universal in range and applicability as any abstraction. We should remind ourselves of Aristotle's dictum:

> The greatest thing by far is to be a master of metaphor. It is the one thing that cannot be learnt from others; and it is also a sign of genius, since a good metaphor implies an intuitive perception of the similarity in dissimilars. (*Poetics* XXII 1459a9)

He may have been thinking of rhetoric, which has deteriorated into propaganda in our day, or poetry, which has become privatized and trivialized. But once we look at the role of metaphor in the public world we will recognize it as truth-revealing and not only truth-concealing and manipulating. While philosophers and scientists have been busy with their abstractions and defending scientism, making the modern technological miracle, politicians and crowd-rousers have been allowed to run free in the fields of metaphor for their own purposes of power.

Without any sacrifice of ethical integrity and without being a poet or a journalist, Wittgenstein was, in the

Aristotelean sense, a "master of metaphor," and when he abandoned the method of abstraction, this power was applied to the task of conceptual clarification. What after all was the new method of "rearrangement of what everybody already knows"? I see it as a method of getting at truth through the self-revealings of *metaphoric connections*. We must not imagine that in straightening out grammar to get rid of philosophic tangles we are restoring some order of grammar that is already there. This would be smuggling metaphysics back in through the back door. Rather what we are doing, in the name of grammar, through freshly seen metaphoric connections, is permitting the sanity and intelligence of everyday humanity to shine through. These are the "rearrangements" that liberate us and are persuasive because of that.

From all accounts it was a heady experience to be in the company of Wittgenstein when he was making his extraordinary connections, or, as he called it, "inventing new similes" (CV 19e), which released the minds of students into new and clarifying changes of context through connecting metaphors.

The End of the Age of Abstraction

We began this book by saying that Wittgenstein's philosophy introduces an epochal change, such a change as happens only every several hundred years. It is possible now to sum up what this change is in this way: "Vertical" hierarchical abstraction, the principal movement of thought for the last 500 years, is replaced in Wittgenstein by "horizontal" metaphoric connections. If we were to look for some symbol of the end of the Age of Abstraction, it might well be Russell's daring but futile Axiom of Infinity.[4] And symbolizing the new situation might be Wittgenstein's statement, discussed above, that a six-year-old boy knows as much about the foundations of arithmetic as Bertrand Russell does.

In comparing Wittgenstein's "new thoughts" with his "old thoughts," to speak now in his language, two pictures collided (in the way that they only can in history): one very strongly entrenched for centuries and the other already all around us though scarcely recognized yet. The old picture is that of a triumphant march toward truth and a better world through increasing abstraction of thought. It is the dream that, before it collapses, turns the world into a paradise-hell, in one respect, and, in another, into a spiritual wasteland.

But once again we have to look more closely. We have not yet realized that the second "picture" is not so weak and ineffectual as it seems. It too has vast antecedents, these ones going back long before the modern world. To take one such ancestral idea, we are reminded of one that stands near the birth of Western civilization, Plato's doctrine of recollection (*anamnesis*), without, of course, its formal otherworldly overtones. And, as we will become increasingly aware, it belongs to religious traditions which have always believed, as Wittgenstein did, that, in the most important sense, we are already, all of us, where we ought to be, and that if we cannot find the main source of truth somewhere in ourselves, we will never find it anywhere else. Wittgenstein reminds us in a most vivid way that abstract functions, which allow us to grasp natural power, should not be allowed to replace essential human activity (which is not technical or pragmatic or ideological) and the normal human intelligence that informs it and is embodied in the grammar of ordinary language.

This indeed is something so familiar and obvious

that few can see it: the daily life that carries on through centuries, through wars and revolutions, catastrophes, rise and fall of empires, technological triumphs and defeats. To say that there is no "power" in this is to restrict that word to adolescent fantasies of war and empire, when, in fact, daily life persists in a way more stable and pervasive and also more fabulous and mysterious than the shouting and arrogance of "power."

How does Wittgenstein stand in relation to the Computer Age, the furthest outcome of the Age of Abstraction which Wittgenstein signals the end of? I want to suggest that the Computer Age, understood correctly, is already on the *other* side of the divide and, although we may not understand this yet, in the Computer the Age of Abstraction has completed its work. This is what Wittgenstein's "externalization of mental processes" is all about. What *can* be computerized *has* to be computerized. Either we are losing our most precious "possession," our "mental inner world," or what we are losing is only a house of cards, which properly can be turned over to the machine, since it has now been recognized as being essentially mechanical after all. Have we not all this time been nine-tenths asleep, like old machines? And is it not now time to wake up to what is not machinelike in us?[5] If what is machinelike ("externalizable") about our "mental processes" is taken away from us and turned over to the computers, that should leave with us what is much more deeply and importantly human: our immediacy, our spontaneity, our joy and our freedom. Let the machines have what belongs to the machines while we have what is genuinely human. It is the attempt to state the latter that is the glory of Wittgenstein's philosophy.

From the masked animal dancers drawn on the walls

of the Cave at Lascaux 30,000 years ago, to the latest intercontinental rockets, we have found a way to imitate and outdo the animals, including the birds and fish. Will we now be able to outdo the machines which we ourselves have made and which are superior to us in so many so-called "mental processes"? Will it be this way: we will make the machines more and more like ourselves, and even better in many respects, until one day we wake up and find that we have become machines ourselves? Or will we discover that we have metamorphosed into something infinitely more real than what we are now?

Notes

Chapter 1   Epochal Change

1. Historically language has been consistently thought of as *in between* human beings and the world, and this is undoubtedly still the prevailing image. For both Heidegger and Wittgenstein, however, language is more like a surrounding "field" within which both "language" and "world" are located, though, as we will see, this is misleadingly over-simplified.

2. We stand today under the spell of "abstraction," the way of thinking from which Wittgenstein in his later philosophy attempted to free himself. The last chapter of this book discusses what is meant by "abstraction" and how Wittgenstein extricated himself from it.

Chapter 2   Limits of Logical Language

1. The painting that is just RED, by showing that color alone, is doubtless "saying" that *nobody sees RED* (or any other immediate sense experience) *but I*, and nothing can take the place of that first-person seeing. A similar point is made, in a much more "philosophical" way, in a famous dual art work in the Philadelphia Museum by Marcel Duchamp. It consists of two parts: (1) a huge ceiling-high "Large Glass" with symbols painted on it depicting, in a more or less humorous way, the public world of shared common symbols, and (2) next to it, but in another gallery, a private "vision," which can be seen by only one viewer at a time looking through a single peephole in an old wooden door. On the one hand is the publically shared world of language and commonly shared symbols, and, on the other, that private experience of firsthand "content," which each individual I has alone. Students of the *Tractatus* will

recognize the Wittgensteinian cast of the Duchamp work, despite the many differences between the witty Frenchman and the intensely serious Austrian.

2. We have in the history of philosophy four main conceptions of "the present": (a) Aristotle's knife-edge present, a mathematically infinitely small limit-point between past and future; (b) Whitehead's "specious present," an indefinite stretch of first-person experienced "presentness"; (c) the empirical present, measurable durations of different consciousness-spans in different animals, the "objective" account; (d) the eternal present, mystic experience of eternity as an "everlasting present": often called the *nunc stasis* (standing now) account.

In Buddhist philosophy and in Heidegger's philosophy "present" means still something different. See, for example, Joan Stambaugh's books comparing Heidegger's conception of time with that of the Zen philosopher, Dogen.

Chapter 3   Breaking the Spell of the Ideal

1. Most people cannot imagine the *passion* which Wittgenstein attached to logical exactitude, giving it almost the sense of a religious mission. Wittgenstein's biographer Brian McGuinness tells the story that when Wittgenstein designed a house for his sister Hermine in Vienna in 1926, it was nearly finished and ready to be cleaned when he decided that the ceiling of one of the rooms (a room large enough to be a hall) had to be raised by *three centimeters*. Even today (when it has been taken over by the Bulgarian government and altered here and there) the house still has a geometrical asceticism, which makes understandable Hermine's statement that it was "too perfect to live in." This is exactly the conclusion that Wittgenstein himself came to about his entire early philosophy: *too perfect to live in.*

2. Wittgenstein said that it is not enough to criticize people or an age; it is necessary to show step-by-step how to get from where we are to where we have to be. In other words, we have to *begin* with an understanding of where people are now—that is, imprisoned in a scientistic abstract way of thinking which he himself mainly shared in the *Tractatus*, though

he had also taken some crucial steps away from it before he wrote even that book. The two phases of Wittgenstein's philosophy have to be studied together because each one sheds a great deal of light on the other.

Chapter 4   Grammar as Deep Culture

1. The change from *essence of description* (isomorphic structural mappings) to *description of essence* (description of language in its aspect of "*possibilities* of meaning") bears a strange resemblance to the change that came about in Heidegger's philosophy at almost the same time. Heidegger described his inability to arrive at the *essence of truth* in the terms that he had laid down in *Being and Time* and how he reversed this to deal with the *truth of essence.* The *meaning of Being,* with which the first book opened, became the *truth of Being,* where "truth" harked back to a rereading of the Greek *aletheia* as *disclosing-and-concealing.*

2. The novelist Saul Bellow in *Mr. Sammler's Planet* expresses the same kind of disgust with the unceasing flood of explaining and explanation that characterizes life today. In one of his Notebooks Wittgenstein bursts out: "When will you leave explaining alone." And Bellow says: "You had to be a crank to insist upon being right. Being right was largely a matter of explanations. Intellectual man had become an explaining creature. Fathers to children, lecturers to listeners, experts to laymen, colleagues to colleagues, doctors to patients, man to his own soul, explained."

Chapter 5   Dimensions of Meaning

1. Because of the relativity of the terms East and West we have arbitrarily chosen to put "East" on the left in the compass diagrams. Think of how we see a map of the United States, then how we see one of the United States and the Pacific Rim. Also think of left and right being reversed in pictures and brain – handedness relations. This could make an excellent model of masculine/feminine relations if we give it a gender-meaning.

2. Wittgenstein wrote: "A phenomenon isn't a symptom of something else. It is the reality." Goethe said it this way: "Do not look for anything behind the phenomena; they are themselves their own lesson." And again Wittgenstein: "Since everything lies open to view, there is nothing to explain."

3. Kripke attempted to restore self-identity by introducing a metaphysical notion of "rigid designators" in his book *Naming and Necessity* (Harvard, 1980).

Chapter 6   Relocating the Self

1. The "inner world" or the "inner facade" refers to the supposed mental objects of introspection, reflection, memory, etc. "Inner life," on the other hand, is what is "born in the soul" or belongs to the "inner conversation" which Wittgenstein, for example, said he carried on with himself (CV 77e). There appears to be something like "language coming to be in us" that has nothing to do with the "inner facade."

2. Julius Weinberg, *Ideas and Concepts* (Milwaukee: 1970). Plato's Forms are either "participated in" or "imitated" in the human mind when we contemplate or think. In Aristotle "intelligible species" are abstracted by the active intellect from "phantasms" received by the senses. Augustine speaks of contents of consciousness as *notio* or *notita*. Since the Renaissance both rationalists and empiricists have accepted the doctrine of "mental contents," disagreeing only on whether some are innate or all come from the senses. If we are able to turn our attention onto something, this has been regarded as sufficient to establish it as a "mental object."

3. See especially Norman Malcolm, *Memory and Mind* (Cornell, 1977), and G. E. M. Anscombe, "The Reality of the Past," in Max Black (ed.) *Philosophical Analysis* (Cornell, 1950).

4. To the mind-boggling dilemmas of solipsism, "My experience alone is real," and "I do not know whether anyone else has what I have when I have direct experiences of the senses," Wittgenstein replies: "You do not *have* them and you do not even *see* them. Language is tricking you into a way of talking that makes it *seem* that *you* have something that no one else has."

5. For a fuller discussion of the private language argument see Chapter 9 in my previous book *Wittgenstein—the Later Philosophy*.

Chapter 7   Return of the Ritual

1. See especially the books by the anthropologist Victor Turner, who was one of the first to work out the connections between theater, performance and ritual.

2. Fingarette points out the way in which contemporary British linguistic philosophy, especially that of J. L. Austin, parallels ancient Confucian ideas.

Chapter 8   Redemption of Action

1. These books will be found helpful with regard to the philosophy of action: Allan R. White (ed.), *The Philosophy of Action* (Oxford, 1968); A. R. Louch, *Explanation and Human Action* (Berkeley: 1966); Irving Thalberg, *Enigmas of Action* (London: 1972); Myles Brand (ed.), *The Nature of Human Action* (Glenview, Ill.: 1970).

2. See John T. E. Richardson, *The Grammar of Justification*, (New York: 1976).

Chapter 9   Entering an Unknown Country

1. G. E. Moore, with the bland childlike innocence which he shared with Russell and which never ceased to flummox Wittgenstein, once remarked that he would like to practice the method that Wittgenstein used, but could never discover what it was. This was rather like the village idiot talking about the village shaman. If we could imagine the shaman's reply, it might be somewhat like what D. H. Lawrence said to Bertrand Russell (which, Russell later confessed, gave him the unhappiest night of his life). He told him not to be so "in his head," in other words, to stop acting like a detached head. Russell's notorious sexual promiscuity not only does not refute this, but by its shameless triviality suggests that Lawrence was right. There is no evidence that Wittgenstein, who was homosexual, was promiscuous, certainly not in his adult life.

Chapter 10 Identity and Identitylessness

1. The Stoic (and some would say also Judaic) idea of freedom is essentially that of Kant, which is that of the *ethical self* or *free will*, in which the self still retains its identity through its capacity to decide. This is to be contrasted with the Christian and Buddhist idea of freedom as the abandonment of all self, *including the self as will*. Kierkegaard linked this last alternative with religious faith. But there is nothing of this in Wittgenstein. Some have confused self with individuality, which of course does not disappear. Both Christ and the Buddha remained, after all, particular individuals.

2. Norman Malcolm's posthumously published *Wittgenstein, a Religious Point of View* (Cornell, 1994) gets into such difficulties by trying to draw analogies between certain of Wittgenstein's philosophical doctrines and some traditional religious views. Thus he overlooks the much more obvious point that the spirit of Wittgenstein was religious through and through in its never-questioned supernaturalism, reverence for all religions and constant struggle with ego and self, not to mention the extreme intellectual humility of being open to so much newness.

Chapter 11 Two Ways of Thinking

1. A most interesting objection raised against the *Principia* is that, even though it purports to give the logical foundations for arithmetic, it makes use of arithmetic in doing this. For example, it may be necessary to *count* the number of parentheses in order to keep the logical formulations intelligible. But making use of *numbers*, which are supposed to have been removed in favor of algebraic symbols, would be an impermissible shoddiness.

2. The historian of mathematics Dirk J. Struik, perhaps recognizing the very un-Greek character of even the first tiny step toward algebra, suggests that Diophantus of Alexandria may have been a Hellenized Babylonian (*Concise History of Mathematics*, I, 74).

3. Nothing better demonstrates the extreme lengths to which abstraction goes in the *Tractatus* than the fact that even today (1995), some seventy-odd years after the first publication of the book, the most serious students are unable to agree on what Wittgenstein meant by the most important metaphysical term in the book, *objects*. When Wittgenstein himself was asked, his answers failed to remove the confusion. Was it an empirical term or a postulate? Something physics might some day supply or something belonging to an eternal super-geometry? The four most popular answers appear to be: (1) an object is a simple sensation or sense data; (2) it is whatever eventually turns out to be the simplest element in physics; (3) it is a point in "logical space," analogous to a point in geometric space; and (4) it is a "divine idea" of a point. My own view is closest to number 3, that objects are what correspond to the coordinates for locating sense qualities in different kinds of "property spaces," in complete analogy to what is done in locating objects in space-time, however many dimensions may be required, etc.

4. The *Axiom of Infinity* illustrates best of all the high point of ideal logical abstractionism reached by Whitehead and Russell in the Universal Algebra of the *Principia Mathematica*. In order to guarantee that there will be an infinity of objects (required by Cantor's set theory) Russell takes *classes* as objects, not only that, but *empty* classes, in case there are no other objects in the universe, and then classes as *classes of classes*, and so on and on. This is one way of "manufacturing objects," by simply wiping out the distinction between imaginary and real. It would seem that logical idealism could go no further! On this papier-mâché rock the project of a Universal Algebra shatters!

There is, of course, also the amazingly complicated proof of another Viennese, Kurt Gödel, that arithmetic can never be "closed" because the assumption that it *is* a closed system can be shown to produce a self-contradiction. I remember when this proof was demonstrated in class by one of its foremost expositors, Ernest Nagel at Columbia in New York. It took Nagel two days to go through the whole thing. By the time we were nearing the end, we had forgotten the beginning. This illustrates one of Wittgenstein's main points with regard to any mathematical "proof" (as with regard to *all* "understanding," we might add) that the "proof" must be *surveyable*—that is, it must be possible to take it all in *in one act of comprehension.* Like the modern corporation or government department, which can no longer be taken in in *a single act of understanding,* even by its own manager, Gödel's proof cannot be taken in. In both cases we have exceeded human limits in a pernicious way. After all, why speak of *one* corporation or *one* department or *one* proof then; why not speak of *two* of each?

5. Two remarkable teachers of the century just ending caught more than a glimpse of the significance of the human "discarding" of age-old machinelike aspects of the human mind, which can now be turned over to computers, thus leaving room for what is human in a much vaster sense than we have ever imagined. These men were about as far apart as possible, though significantly both were outside the Western metaphysical tradition. They were Eric Gutkind (1877–1965) and Georg Ivanovitch Gurdjieff (1872–1949). Gutkind was the author of *Body of God,* published posthumously in 1969, and a profound student of the Jewish Kabbala, particularly of Isaac Luria (1534–1572). Gurdjieff, in some ways the most extraordinary man of our time, was the author of *All and Everything: Beelzebub's Tales to His Grandson* (New York: 1950) and *Meetings with Remarkable Men* (New York: 1970), his teaching deriving from ancient Middle Eastern and Sufi sources. As luck would have it, one day in October 1949 I was in the Great Hall of the Cooper Union in New York for a lecture by the famous architect Frank Lloyd Wright. He came out on the stage and began his lecture with these words, which are imprinted on my memory: "The greatest man of our time has died today, and probably none of you have ever heard of him." It was Gurdjieff, and I think he was right: nobody *had* heard of him.

Appendices

The most terrible and awful error of our age is the fact that language is assumed to be sufficient for mutual understanding.

Frederick van Eeden

Appendix 1 Wittgenstein's Reading

In one of the most illuminated sections of *Philosophical Investigations* Wittgenstein tells us that reading is not "psychological," but if we understand the meaning of the word deeply enough, which means in the full range of its relations to other words, we will know all there is to know about reading.

He described his own method of reading as being *very slow* and said that this is how he would like his own writings to be read. The motto that in philosophy "the winner is he who finishes last" (CV 34e) applies to reading also.

For a "great" philosopher, Wittgenstein read extraordinarily little philosophy. He said he had never read a word of Aristotle. But he did read Plato and particularly the *Theaetetus*. He also read St. Augustine's *Confessions* and especially admired Berkeley and Kant (though we do not know how much of them he read, probably little). He found Schopenhauer superficial, very much admired Kierkegaard, though later on found him too repetitious to read, read "excerpts" from St. John of the Cross, gave copies of Dr. Johnson's *Prayers* to his friends and benefited greatly from reading William James's *Varieties of Religious Experience*. Above all, he admired Tolstoi's later religious parables (about peasant life) and Dostoievsky's *Brothers Karamazov*, which he evidently read many times. Among his other favorite authors and books were Gottfried Keller's *Green Henry*, Laurence Sterne's *Tristram Shandy* and Georg Lichtenberg's *Aphorisms*. He had dipped into but was somewhat critical of Charles Dickens and Jane Austen, for original and interesting reasons.

In general, as his biographer Brian McGuinness points out, "Wittgenstein nowhere discusses an author he does not respect," even though he may be critical of him or her. The great writers Goethe, Schiller, Mörike, Lessing, he "turned to all his life." But it is very characteristic that he also supported the avant-garde of his time. When, under the influence of Tolstoi and the idea of voluntary poverty, he decided to give away his vast inherited fortune through his friend the literary editor Ludwig Ficker, he and Ficker gave it to struggling young poets and artists (seventeen of them). The three main beneficiaries were poets of superior genius: Rainer Maria Rilke, Georg Trakl and Carl Dallago. Trakl, an especially extraordinary poet (about whom Heidegger wrote one of his greatest essays), killed himself at the age of twenty-six on the Russian front during the First World War by an overdose of cocaine. When it was realized that Trakl was in desperate straits (as a mere pharmacist, he had had to watch ninety men entrusted to his care die in agony without being able to do anything for them because of the shortage of drugs), Wittgenstein was sent for by Ficker, but arrived two days too late.

Another figure that haunts the pages of *Culture and Value* is Shakespeare. What Wittgenstein had to say about him, as we might expect, is memorable. Shakespeare, he said, was not a poet. He could not be thought of in that category on a par with other great poets. He was instead something like a force of nature, the "spirit of the English language." Though he was not a moral force (like Beethoven), it was as if the English language used him as a mouthpiece (CV 83e–86e). (Shakespeare, incidentally, is said to have been Beethoven's idol, a fact not noted by Wittgenstein.)

Also very important in Wittgenstein's reading was the New Testament. He knew it well enough so that he could tell his friend Drury that he didn't like the Epistle of Peter (but wasn't aware that it wasn't written by Peter) and that he preferred Matthew to the other Gospels. His attitude toward the Christian Bible as a whole, as revealed in the *Culture and Value* extracts, was conventional enough: that the Old Testament was the "body," the New Testament was the "head," and he wasn't sure that we needed the "crown," Paul's Letters.

But on Paul, as on Karl Barth, he seems to have changed his mind. At first in a Tolstoian way, he felt that the Gospels were enough; then later he said that perhaps after all Paul wrote in the same spirit; he would have to defer to those who knew more about it than he did. (In religion and in matters of aesthetic taste he would defer to others, but never in philosophy!) When Drury, at his request, first read aloud to him from writings of the Protestant theologian Karl Barth, he put a stop to it, saying that all he could hear was "arrogance." But then later, having seemingly forgotten this episode, he suddenly recommended Barth to Drury. When Drury reminded him of his earlier reaction, he was conspicuously silent.

The two main religious writers for him were Tolstoi and Dostoievsky. At times we get the impression that he couldn't decide between them, during World War I reading Tolstoi's *The Kingdom of God is Among You* and, while working as a village schoolteacher in Austria, reading the *Brothers Karamazov* again and again. We also get the impression that in the end Tolstoi's sanity and naturalness came first, especially toward the end of Wittgenstein's life when Tolstoi's *Twenty-three Tales* dealing with the religion of the peasants became his favorite.

How did Wittgenstein feel about not reading the great philosophers? The contrast with Heidegger is striking, for Heidegger read everything in the history of philosophy and wrote about it all—the pre-Socratics, Plato, Aristotle (in full), the medievals including Duns Scotus and William of Occam, Meister Eckhart, Spinoza and Leibniz (perhaps not the English empiricists), Kant and Hegel (both of whom he wrote about at length), Kierkegaard, Husserl, and Nietzsche (three volumes on him).

Wittgenstein, we would have to say, was a-historical. He was possessed of the *geometrical spirit* (as Pascal described it) and had little interest in narrative or history. Where Heidegger saw philosophy as the movement along a forest path (and the clearing was the *present*), Wittgenstein saw it as the *synoptic view*, as it were from a mountain top. If these are two different "ways of understanding," then we are not surprised that they are reflected in the different reading patterns.

We are fortunate that the philosopher Karl Britton has given us a description of how Wittgenstein felt about reading philosophy. Britton writes of Wittgenstein's rooms in Whewell Court in Cambridge:

> There were seldom any philosophical books to be seen. And indeed Wittgenstein in those days often warned us against reading philosophical books. If we took a book seriously, he would say, it ought to puzzle us so much that we would throw it across the room and think about the problems for ourselves. (*Listener,* June 16, 1955)

In Wittgenstein's view we will not find clues for answers in the traditional writings, great as they were (and he always insisted on the greatness of the great philosophers). Paradoxically, his sense of changing history was so strong that he did not find them relevant. For Heidegger, on the other hand, the *origin* was ever present and this was indubitably historic. Not a geometric layout, but living origins, always showing themselves, was what he valued.

Wittgenstein felt that it was also good that he had not allowed himself to be too much influenced by other thinkers, past as well as present. But at the same time he was conscious of the extent to which his main ideas had come from the few other sources that had mattered greatly to him, which he recalled during his life again and again. In one of these moments he listed in his notebooks the thinkers who had influenced him the most. There were ten of them and he listed them in the order in which he had read them. We can learn a great deal from this list because there are unexpected confluences of ideas which return again and again in different forms in Wittgenstein's philosophy. It is as if these were *talismans*, constantly available as landmarks set in the ground to which he was always able to refer. The very first book on the list, for example, Boltzmann, focuses on the idea of multiplicities of points of view equally valid in science, an eerie anticipation of the multiplicity of language-games in philosophy, while the second book, Hertz's *Principles of Mechanics*, envisages a geometrical mechanics without the idea of *force* and also thinks of scientific concepts as "pictures," both ideas central in the *Tractatus*.

(1) *Ludwig Boltzmann* (1844–1906), *Populäre Schriften* (1906). Theoretical physicist LW intended to study with, but Boltzmann committed suicide in 1906. He defended the idea of multiple theories for the same facts, all equally correct.

(2) *Heinrich Hertz* (1857–1894), *Principles of Mechanics* (1899). Scientific concepts as "pictures of things." "The whole task of philosophy is to give such a form to our expression that certain disquietudes or problems vanish."

(3) *Arthur Schopenhauer* (1788–1860), *World as Will and Idea* (1818). "World is my idea"—solipsist implications and *will* as reality. LW later critical of him; said "Schopenhauer never searches his conscience" (CV 36).

(4) *Gottlob Frege* (1848–1925), *Sinn und Bedeutung (Sense and Reference)* (1892). Developed propositional calculus and derived arithmetic from logic. Meaning dependent on truth conditions. Kantian epistemology not integrated with logic. LW considered him a "great thinker."

(5) *Bertrand Russell* (1872–1970), *Principia Mathematica* (1910–1913). With Whitehead developed symbolic logic.

Logical atomist. Identified methods of philosophy with those of science. Early supported Wittgenstein at Cambridge, but rejected W's later philosophy.

(6) *Karl Kraus* (1874–1936) single-handedly wrote *Die Fackel (The Torch)* (1911–1936), satirical journal, defending German language and seeing in the depths of grammar the only valid morality. Exercised great influence as independent thinker in Vienna.

(7) *Adolf Loos* (1870–1933), Viennese architect, stressing purity and functionalism. Despised ornamentation and pretense. LW's own architectural design of a house in Vienna for his sister (Barkgasse 18, 1926) followed Loos's principles to an even greater degree of geometrical severity. House now owned by Bulgarian government.

(8) *Otto Weininger* (1880–1903), *Sex and Character* (1903). In his one book linked misogyny and anti-Semitism. Also presented alternative: *Genius or death.* Killed himself in house where Beethoven died. LW recommended him to G. E. Moore, though thought him wrong-headed.

(9) *Oswald Spengler* (1880–1936), *Decline of the West* (1918). Highly influential morphology of history. LW admired him but was critical of his methodology. His prediction of "coming Caesarism" not echoed in LW.

(10) *Piero Sraffa* (1898–1975), *Production of Commodities by Means of Commodities* (1960). Marxist revisionist economist. LW attributed his own "most consequential" PI ideas to Sraffa's stimulus.

To this list may be added a few other names of writers who might be described as Wittgenstein's *spiritual companions:*

Gottfried Keller (1819–1890), author of *Green Henry;*
Leo Tolstoi (1828–1910), especially later religious parables;
Fyodor Dostoievsky (1821–1881), read *Brothers Karamazov* many times;
Georg Lichtenberg (1742–1799), quoted his *Aphorisms;*
J. W. von Goethe (1749–1832) on theory of color and physiognomy;

Samuel Johnson (1709–1784), *Prayers*;
William James (1842–1910), *Principles of Psychology* and
Varieties of Religious Experience.

One last statistic: A *Wittgenstein Bibliography*, published
in 1989, edited by V. A. and S. G. Shanker, lists *5868 books
and articles* dealing with some aspect or another of
Wittgenstein's philosophy, and more than 500 persons and
topic entries in attached Index. All this about a philosopher
who did not believe in philosophy as a profession.

Appendix 2 Wittgenstein's Politics

As a philosopher Wittgenstein refused to belong to "any
community of ideas," and this included any political or religious, fraternal or professional organizations or institutions. He
had no use for partisan politics or sectarianism. And his thinking did not fall into the categories of "left" or "right," or "believ-
er" or "non-believer." There were no emotional identifications
of those sorts, which so often betray lesser philosophers. He
seemed to scorn equally both conservatives and liberals.

Many commentators have pointed out Wittgenstein's great
respect for authority and, of course, ancient authority, for
example, the Church. (He would have greatly admired
Confucius, at least the Confucius described by Herbert
Fingarette in the chapter on ritual in this book.) Karl Britton
described him as a great admirer of Bismarck, whom he liked
to talk about. At the same time the man to whom he attributed
his greatest intellectual stimulation at Cambridge during the last
dozen years of his life was the neo-Marxist economist Piero
Sraffa, friend of the imprisoned Italian Communist leader
Antonio Gramsci, whom Wittgenstein tried to have released.
These facts should make it clear that Wittgenstein had no ideological attachments, in an age when ideology raged everywhere. Like Simone Weil he despised the collective mania of
the Great Beast.

The proper description that seems to apply to him is the combination, perhaps only to be found in Vienna, of an *arch-traditionalist* and a member of the *avant-garde*, a combination not eclectic or dilettantish, but fused together by an intense moral passion. More specifically, an enormous respect for tradition was combined with a Tolstoian yearning for equality, which, like Tolstoi, he attempted to put into practice, with somewhat analogous consequences. (When Tolstoi announced that he intended to renounce all copyright royalties on his books and make them all available free to everybody to reprint at will, his wife became hysterical in her opposition. When Wittgenstein distributed his fortune to young artists and poets, his brother, the great one-handed pianist Paul Wittgenstein, refused to speak to him again and many years later would not even speak to a friend of Ludwig's, the great mathematician, Brouwer, when he accidentally encountered him in New York.)

We cannot say the ultraconservative and the religious anarchist-antinomian were harmoniously joined in Wittgenstein (any more than they were in Heidegger or in Simone Weil) but they lived together in him, and this helps to shed light on a much discussed remark he once made to his friend M. O'C. Drury:

> I am not a religious man, but I cannot help seeing every problem from a religious point of view.

The first part of this sentence means that he did not belong to any religious institution and did not follow any religious practice regularly (though there were periods when he prayed regularly). The second part means (it seems to me) that the religious point of view and the philosophic point of view were fused in him in the sense that they both involved the same kind of intellectual humility and radical inner openness. (A different understanding is put forward in Norman Malcolm's posthumous book *Wittgenstein—A Religious Point of View* [Cornell, 1994]. Wittgenstein had a religious spirit, which helps to account for his vehement rejection of scientism.)

It is against this background that we can begin to under-

stand why Wittgenstein despised Bertrand Russell's liberalism
and pacifism. (He told a friend that Russell's writings on logic
and mathematics should be bound in blue and made required
reading, while his writings on social problems should be bound
in red and forbidden to be read.) Russell's views must have
seemed paper-thin to someone who valued ancient tradition as
much as Wittgenstein did. Wittgenstein was all his life, we must
remember, a supernaturalist like Pascal and Dostoievsky, while
Russell remained a scientific utilitarian. (Russell once spent an
evening with D. H. Lawrence, which, according to Russell's
own account, almost resulted in his suicide, so deeply did
Lawrence shake his faith in science and reason. It was the can-
dor with which Russell could tell such things about himself that
Wittgenstein put the most value on—that and Russell's incredi-
bly fast and brilliant mind.) The closest Russell got to religion in
Wittgenstein's sense was when he recommended Spinoza's pan-
theistic vision for its tranquillizing affect! Russell's opinion of
Wittgenstein's later work was that his erstwhile student turned
mentor had given up philosophy, while Wittgenstein remarked
of Russell's later efforts that "Russell ran out of problems."

It would never have occurred to Russell, or at least would
never have seemed of any philosophic interest if it had, that his
vanity and pride could have anything to do with philosophy or
his philosophy. We might say that his philosophy remained
cerebral. This verged on the cleverness that Wittgenstein disliked so intensely in British philosophy, to the point where he
avoided eating in the Trinity Dining Hall because he so disliked
the game the Trinity dons played in trying to score off each
other. Philosophy was much too serious for Wittgenstein to be
coupled with this kind of witty badinage. On numerous occasions he made it very clear that he much preferred real silliness
(Wodehouse, Lewis Carroll, Edward Lear) to the Cambridge
cleverness and academic one-upmanship. (The class overtones
of this could only have further disgusted him, since, belonging
to one of the richest families in Vienna and then giving it all up,
he was not in any awe of superior class tones and manners.)

Russell (he was then Lord Russell), for his part, maintained the superior tone which his work in abstract logic some-how validated. If he thought that perhaps there was something too fanatical in Wittgenstein's very intensity, which had at first enthralled him so, good taste forbade making much of it. Russell's cerebral icy logic was melted into something far more human in Wittgenstein's later philosophy, but it is far too soon to see what effect this will have on the long-term development of British philosophy itself.

In the meantime we can get a good summary of Wittgenstein's two perhaps strongest "political" feelings by looking at his reaction to the atom bomb in 1936: (1) dislike of the liberal-pacifist reaction ("the philistines"), and (2) equal dis-like of our "horrible" and "disgusting" modern science which had produced such a thing.

> The hysterical fear over the atom bomb now being experi-enced, or at any rate expressed, by the public almost sug-gests that at last something really salutary has been invented. The fright at least gives the impression of a real-ly effective bitter medicine. I can't help thinking: if this didn't have something good about it, the *philistines* wouldn't be making an outcry. But perhaps this too is a childish idea. Because really all I can mean is that the bomb offers a prospect of the end, the destruction, of a horrible evil—our disgusting dish-watery science. And certainly that's not an unpleasant thought; but who can say what would come *after* this destruction? The people now making speeches against producing the bomb are undoubtedly the *scum* of the intellectuals, but even that does not prove beyond question that what they abomi-nate is to be welcomed. (CV 48e–49e)

Among those speaking against the bomb, of course, was Russell, who could hardly be called a philistine. One wonders if, in his revulsion against what he apparently regarded as the sloppy-headedness of liberals and pacifists, Wittgenstein had forgotten that Russell had gone to jail for his convictions in World War I.

Appendix 3 Vienna and Karl Kraus

It has been said that the greatest number of important cultural movements of the twentieth century were born in *fin de siècle* Vienna (that is, around 1900), thus putting Vienna of that time in a class with fourth-century B.C. Athens and fifteenth-century Florence (some would add Elizabethan London) as a place and time of greatest intellectual ferment. They were all place-times where one could not "throw a stone without hitting a genius."

The claim seems justified when one looks into some recent books on Vienna-1900, such as William Johnston's *The Austrian Mind* (Berkeley: 1972) Carl Schorske's *Fin de Siècle Vienna* (New York: 1980) and Allan Janik and Stephen Toulmin's *Wittgenstein's Vienna* (New York: 1973). What we find is that Vienna was the birthplace of Nazism (Hitler, H. S. Chamberlain, Lueger) and Zionism (Herzl and Buber); psychoanalysis, (Freud, Adler, Rank); modern music (Bruckner, Mahler, Schönberg, Webern and Berg); philosophical theoretical physics (Boltzmann, Herz, Mach, Neurath); sociology of knowledge (Lukacs, Mannheim, Schumpeter, Kelsen); and a great deal of important literature and poetry (Musil, Broch, Wasserman, Zweig, Werfel, Hofmannsthal, Trakl, Rilke); philosophy (Brentano, Popper, Husserl, Wittgenstein) and art (Kokoschka, Klimt, Loos).

For any modernist it is an impressive roll call. Oddly, nothing that we read about the city gives us any idea why such a ferment should have come about. It was a city of "Schlag and Schmalz" ("Cream and Kitsch" or "Operettas with Whipped Cream"). Waltzing day and night (Frances Trollope, the British authoress, called waltzing a "passion" there even as far back as 1837); idolatry of musicians who had been treated intolerably during their lifetimes, like Mozart, Beethoven and Schubert, and suicide as an aesthetic gesture of heroic ethical decision, leading to the highest suicide rate in Europe. (Three of Wittgenstein's four brothers killed themselves; Ludwig was the youngest in a family of eight children.)

When scholars look around for some one person to sym-
bolize the whole Viennese scene, they often single out the
lonely isolated figure of a one-man critic and gadfly writer-edi-
tor Karl Kraus, who was located somewhere near the epicenter
of the intellectual storm. Satirist and ironist, always ready to
prick the bubble of pretension and hot air, Kraus put out his
broadside paper *Die Fackel (The Torch)* for 37 years and 922
issues, virtually single-handedly. But he was more than a gadfly. All the others whose names we have mentioned have come
into their own in the century just ending, *except for Kraus and
Wittgenstein, whose day is still to come.*

Kraus was very representative, not the least in being a
Jew, for Jews played an important part in the intellectual ferment. He was, like so many others in Vienna, an assimilated
Jew, converting to Catholicism, as did, for example, Mahler,
Broch, Werfel, Neurath and Adler. Kraus summed up the
Jewish situation around him when he said that Jews were
"fated to dissolve entirely into their surrounding culture and yet
nevertheless remain a ferment." (See Steven Beller, *Vienna
and the Jews, 1867–1938* [Cambridge, 1989].)

Kraus was a profound influence on Wittgenstein not for
his political or cultural views, but for his ideas about language,
which were accompanied by an ear for the nuances of language probably unmatched by any other writer of German of
his time. If Wittgenstein learned his marvellous literary style
from anyone, it must have been from Kraus, though Frege
played a part.

Just how deep Kraus's sensitivity to language went has
been stated by his English translator J. P. Stern. Speaking of
Kraus, Stern writes:

> Gradually, after 1905, it is borne upon him that lan-
> guage—that is, the way a statement is made—bears within
> itself *all* the signs he needs to understand the moral and
> ethical quality of that statement and of him who made it.
> Conversely, it is only necessary to read a statement in a

> way that is supremely sensitive to all its linguistic qualities
> in order to discover its truth . . . if only you understand
> the grammar of a language well enough, you will find that
> lies are . . . violations of the grammar, that is, of the spirit
> of that language. (*Modern Language Review*, 1966)

Here before the First World War is perhaps the germ of
Wittgenstein's later conception of *grammar*, though stated in
another way.

What do these enigmatic remarks mean? I am reminded of
a Taoist book which made the point that, listening very carefully, it is always possible to tell whether a person is lying or not.
It is revealed not only in the tone of voice but in the actual
configuration of words. A careful reading or listening will pick
out slight awkwardnesses of word choice, words that stand
out, that reveal, for example, the intention of hiding something,
or if not that, a certain uneasiness about what is being said.
Just as a child when it lies gives telltale indications to the par-
ent, so the adult speaker or writer leaves tiny traces, which the
skilled interpreter learns to pick up, as Kraus did. Kraus made
himself a specialist at close reading. He could sense the single
word or sentence in which a writer gave himself or herself
away. If it were a misjudgment or mistake, this would be as
telltale as anything else. The implication was that, since most
human beings do not use much care in speaking and writing,
their language will inevitably betray them and manifest much
more than they mean to say. Stern adds:

> If writers and speakers fully realized what they say and
> write, if they saw and felt the full impact of the verbal
> reality that inheres in their words and has only to be
> uncovered to make its effect, then they would write and
> speak differently and indeed live differently. (*ibid.*)

Appendix 4 Wittgenstein and Buddhism

In my earlier book *Wittgenstein—the Later Philosophy* I included an Appendix in which I pointed out an important similarity between Wittgenstein and Buddhism: the repudiation in both of them of the absolute object and the absolute subject. This referred mainly to the Madhyamika tradition, but also to Zen.

Since then Chris Gudmunsen's book *Wittgenstein and Buddhism* (New York, 1977) has been published, and reading that in conjunction with study of the great Buddhist philosopher Nagarjuna has made me more aware of the struggle in that branch of Buddhism (Madhyamika) to escape from metaphysics, a struggle paralleled in Wittgenstein, and leading to a strangely similar result.

Thus Gudmunsen quotes Frederick Streng's book *Emptiness: A Study in Religious Meaning* (Nashville, 1967):

> The awareness of "emptiness" is not a blank loss of consciousness, an inanimate empty space; rather it is the cognition of daily life without the attachment to it. It is an awareness of distinct entities, of the self, of "good" and "bad" and other practical determinations; but it is aware of these as empty structures. Wisdom is not to be equated with mystical ecstasy; it is rather, the joy of freedom in everyday existence. (Gudmunsen, 103)

Gudmunsen compares Russell's philosophy to the Abhidharma tradition as this was discussed by Wittgenstein's student K. N. Jayatilleke in his book *Early Buddhist Theory of Knowledge* (London, 1963). This may be thought of as a kind of *logical purgation* for the Madhyamika, somewhat as Wittgenstein's early philosophy was a kind of logical purgation for his later detachment from metaphysics.

Nagarjuna's rejection of metaphysics is a kind of wiping of the slate clean through the method known as the *Four-fold Negation*, which applies as well to Western as to Eastern thought. Thus, he says, speaking of what cannot be spoken of (and I add the Western representatives of each alternative, of course unknown to him): It neither is (Aristotle), nor is not (Sceptics), *nor* both is *and* is not (Hegel), nor *neither* is *nor* is not (Plotinus). This would appear to exhaust the alternatives. The result is emptiness or *sunyata*, which may still have a faintly metaphysical ring until we realize that this is simply everyday life, without attachment to (or identification with) anything.

The traditional Buddhist formulation conveying the point that the "world of appearances" is finally seen to coincide with the "absolute emptiness" is *samsara is nirvana* (i.e., the wheel of existence is ultimately seen to be the same as the bliss of release from it). What takes us out of both metaphysics and the opposition to metaphysics is ordinary existence.

We might also say that the world of abstraction in which Westerners live is at the opposite pole from the supreme Buddhist experience of total concrete immediacy (an immediacy greater than any immediacy we know). Technology and everything that goes with it *has no present*. And people who live in that world live in a ghost world without a present. Buddhism, like original Christianity, points to the freedom of immediacy, spontaneity and presentness. What we call ordinary life, if it were accepted in the right spirit, would be this.

Appendix 5 Knots and Keys

Wittgenstein's philosophy leans heavily on metaphors, two in particular having central roles: logical pictures and language-games. (It is interesting that both were suggested by events in the actual world: the first by the drawing of an accident used in a Paris law court, and the second by an impromptu ballgame he saw some boys playing.) We cannot think of Wittgenstein's philosophy without these metaphors, which shows how important new metaphors are in new philosophies.

There are also, however, minor metaphors produced as it were along the way, which if we take the trouble to examine, may illuminate more obscure matters.

Two such are *knots* and *keys*. The knots metaphor is found in *Philosophical Remarks* paragraph 2:

> Why is philosophy so complicated? It ought, after all, to be *completely* simple. Philosophy unties the knots in our thinking, which we have tangled up in an absurd way; but to do that it must make movements which are just as complicated as the knots. Although the result of philosophy is simple, its methods for striving there cannot be so. (PR 52)

This passage gives a certain impression, as if the difficulty were primarily one of complication, whereas something else may enter in, which only appears if we have not a simple knot, but something more like a whole tangled ball of string. We keep thinking as we pull apart each tangle that we have straightened the whole tangle out, only to find each time that there is more to do. Wittgenstein said that it was like this with philosophic problems: we keep imagining that we have removed the tangle, only to find that there is still more to do. We get, as it were, to the more central difficulties or the deeper aspects of the problems.

> Human beings are entangled all unknowing in the net of language. (PI 462)

The metaphor of the key has to do with Wittgenstein's procedure in his own writing. Since this is truly obscure, not to say arcane, it may be better to quote it in full. He is talking about his planned Foreword for *Philosophical Remarks*:

> The danger in a long foreword is that the spirit of the book has to be evident in the book itself and cannot be described. For if a book has been written for just a few readers, that will be clear just from the fact that only a few people understand it. The book must automatically separate those who understand it from those who do not. Even the foreword is written just for those who under-

stand the book. Telling someone something he does not
understand is pointless even if you add that he will not be
able to understand it. (That so often happens with someone you love.) If you have a room which you do not want
certain people to get into, put a lock on it for which they
do not have the key. But there is no point in talking to
them about it, unless of course you want them to admire
the room from outside. The honorable thing to do is to
put a lock on the door which will be noticed by those
who can open it, not by the rest. But it is proper to say
that I think the book has nothing to do with the progressive civilization of Europe and America. (CV 7e)

The question that inevitably comes up here is: Granted that it is
pointless and foolish to encourage people to read something
that we know in advance they will not understand, do we have
to go so far as to put "locks" on it and withold keys? Perhaps
the answer is that Wittgenstein wishes to distinguish between
those who at least will try to understand and those who will
immediately attack the book in a belligerent spirit on the basis
of their initial misunderstanding. It is the second group that
have to be kept out so that, in a way, they will not even get a
foothold to express their preconceived prejudices. Wittgenstein
had had enough of this second group from those who labelled
him a positivist without having understood anything at all,
while totally sure that they were right. The "lock" would say:
*Partisan preconception not wanted. Serious investigators
always welcome.*

We suggested in the Preface to this book that when misunderstandings may do positive harm, ways should be found
to avoid them in the first place, perhaps by withholding certain
clues which would be the most likely to be misunderstood by
those with closed minds. But there may also be a second reason, which arises from Wittgenstein's conception of philosophy. That is his strong conviction that each person has to
understand for him or herself; nobody else can understand for
us. *Understanding is not transferable in the way that knowledge*

is. The hidden keys remind us of that. If you are not disposed to understand, you will not find the keys. (We are at this point reminded of Kierkegaard, whose many pseudonyms were introduced to bring about an "indirect communication" so that readers would not succumb to the idea that it is possible to communicate about matters of faith directly to another person who does not have that "key" of faith.) Those who, like the Wittgenstein scholar J. M. Hunter, believe that Wittgenstein deliberately created "conundrums," may have missed the point that these were "tests" or "roadblocks" to stand in the way of those who were not really serious about making the extra efforts necessary to understand somebody like Wittgenstein.

There is a Sufi story telling of a Sufi *pir* or teacher who was asked by a student why he did not explain the meaning of his stories more clearly, particularly since these meanings seemed to be so well hidden. The teacher replied: "How would you feel if you asked me for an orange, and I gave you one that had already been sucked dry?"

Bibliography

All books are by Ludwig Wittgenstein. Abbreviations are those used in text.

BB   *The Blue and Brown Books.* (Oxford: Blackwell, 1958).

CV   *Culture and Value,* edited by G. H. von Wright in collaboration with Heikki Nyman; translated by Peter Winch. (Chicago: Univ. of Chicago, 1980).

LC   *Lectures and Conversations on Aesthetics, Psychology and Religious Belief,* edited by Cyril Barrett. (Oxford: Blackwell, 1968).

LFM   *Lectures on the Foundations of Mathematics.* From the Notes of R. G. Bosanquet, Norman Malcolm, Rush Rhees and Yorick Smythies. Edited by Cora Diamond. (Ithaca: Cornell, 1976).

N   *Notebooks 1914–1916,* edited by G. H. von Wright and G. E. M. Anscombe, translated by G. E. M. Anscombe. (Oxford: Blackwell, 1961).

OC   *On Certainty,* edited by G. E. M. Anscombe and G. H. von Wright, translated by D. Paul and G. E. M. Anscombe. (Oxford: Blackwell, 1969).

PG   *Philosophical Grammar,* edited by Rush Rhees, translated by Anthony Kenny. (Oxford: Blackwell, 1974).

PI   *Philosophical Investigations,* edited by G. E. M. Anscombe and R. Rhees, translated by G. E. M. Anscombe. (Oxford: Blackwell, 1953).

PO   *Philosophical Occasions,* edited by James C. Klagge and Alfred Nordmann. (Indianapolis and Cambridge: Hackett, 1993).

PR   *Philosophical Remarks,* edited by G. E. M. Anscombe and R. Rhees, translated by G. E. M. Anscombe. (Oxford: Blackwell, 1953).

RFGB   *Remarks on Frazer's "Golden Bough,"* edited by Rush Rhees. (Retford: Brynmill, 1979).

T   *Tractatus Logico-Philosophicus*, translated by D. F. Pears and B. F. McGuinness with an Introduction by Bertrand Russell. (London: Routledge & Kegan Paul, 1961).

Z   *Zettel*, edited by G. E. M. Anscombe and G. H. von Wright, translated by G. E. M. Anscombe. (Berkeley: Univ. of Calif., 1967)

Index

Subjects